Ukrainian Whitework

BY GAY EATON

ISBN No 0-476-01493-X.

© 2005 Gay Eaton

Research: Gay Eaton.

Photography: Michael Hanytsky (page 78); all others by Gay Eaton.

Computer diagrams and illustrations: Gay Eaton.

Embroidered examples: Gay Eaton

Layout and prepress: Hughes Lithographics Ltd, Dunedin

Printed by: Tablet Print, Dunedin.

Published and distributed by Gay Eaton.

Typeset in Adobe Caslon Pro (10.5/13 pt), Myriad Pro (10.25/12.5 pt), and Avalon (headings) using Adobe InDesign CS, Macromedia Freehand 10, and Adobe Photoshop 7 on an Apple iMac G4.

Front cover: Patterns—Anna, Band Sampler, Hala, Lavender Bag (Mychajlo). Ukrainian Easter eggs kindly loaned by Iryna Osipova.

Back cover: Patterns—Band Sampler, Hala, Lavender Bag (Olya), and needle book (Orion).

Acknowledgements

Many have helped me in various ways to research this little known technique and to prepare this book for publication. I would particularly like to thank the following people and acknowledge their generous support, help, enthusiasm and keen interest for Ukrainian Whitework and the story that it tells.

I am indebted to Orion Wenhrynowycz and Michael (Mychajlo) Hanytsky of Melbourne for their unstinting valuable help in sourcing information, sending books, photographs and answering my many questions about their country's history and culture. Allowing their stories and family stories to be included gives us all an insight into what had previously been hidden. This book would not have been written without their sterling support and keen interest.

Other members of the Australian Ukrainian community have also helped in many ways and I am most grateful to them all. Peter Kardash sent a copy of his beautiful book *Ukraine Its History and Its Arts*. Maria Duma and her family, Hala Petreshyn and Halyna Glouchowera, have sent information and answered queries and generously allowed their stories to be included. Lidia Rostek has given much helpful information on their whitework.

I am most grateful to Marge Cross for introducing me to Orion Wenhrynowycz and Michael Hanytsky and the Ukrainian Arts and Crafts Museum, Melbourne. Without that contact with the Australian Ukrainian community this book would not have been possible.

It was because of the encouragement and enthusiasm from my students around New Zealand and Victoria, Australia for Ukrainian Whitework that I decided to prepare this book and give lovers of counted thread needlework an opportunity to enjoy this stunning and little known technique.

MagnumMac, Dunedin, and Owen Baxter have given me much help with my computer and taken me carefully over some of the steep learning curves that I have needed to negotiate.

Semco Craft (NZ) Ltd supplied me with a very generous amount of their excellent linen and thread.

D.M.C. gave permission to include a pattern from their booklet *Openwork Embroidery*. The inclusion of this is important; it gives a link between the little that had previously been shown in West European needlework books.

My proof stitchers Sheila Buck, Noeline Staton, Lesley McIntosh and Stina Mooynan have carefully and willingly undertaken the important task of checking and working the patterns from the drawn graphs.

I am grateful to Jim Swann, Tablet Print, Dunedin, for his enthusiastic support, cheerful encouragement and good advice.

Claire Stevens, Tablet Print has proof read the text and put me back on the right track when needed. She has taken special interest in this book because as a little girl she was tutored by family friend and neighbour, Miss Helen M. Moran (see page 15).

Anne Tamati, Hughes Lithographics, put a lot of careful consideration and graphic skill into designing the cover that reflects the content.

Without the skill and expertise of Graeme McKinstry, Hughes Lithographics, Dunedin this book would not have the stylish layout and presentation that it has. I have been privileged to have him teach me to draw the graphics and to prepare this manuscript and most of the layout for publication.

Lastly none of this would have happened without the support, time and space given to me by my husband Neil.

Ukraine

Capital: Kyviv
Second largest European country.
Population (2002): 49.5 million.
Rich in natural resources:
Fertile plains (steppes), plateaus, mountains
(Carpathians) and Crimea Peninsula.
Farming, forest and woodland, fishing.

Contents

Introduction

Needlework has taken me along many fascinating journeys of discovery, none as diverse as Ukrainian Whitework. Before setting out to prepare this book I knew very little about Ukraine, its history, people and culture, other than it had been under the harsh hammer and sickle rule of the USSR. The journey began while searching for little known techniques to offer as workshops at the Otago Embroiderers' Guild annual School of Embroidery held each March in Wanaka, Central Otago, New Zealand. It was while in Melbourne my friend Marge Cross took me to the Ukrainian Arts and Crafts Museum. The curators, Orion Wenhrynowycz and Michael Hanytsky confirmed that the piece I was working on from the 'D.M.C. Library Openwork Embroidery' booklet, was Ukrainian Whitework and were astounded that I was teaching this technique in New Zealand.

While working the Ukrainian whitework patterns I wanted to know more about the people who enjoyed wearing the richly patterned clothing they had embroidered for themselves and family. The more I read about them the more I wanted to include something of their experiences that have not been generally known in the west. Each pattern is named for a Ukrainian and includes a little of that person's story. The stories give just a glimpse into the horrific, terrifying times that they had to live through. I am most grateful to be given the privilege of including a little of their story with each pattern and know that this was not at all easy to give, as it brought back memories of exceptionally harsh times. Their courage and determination to survive and to ensure that they and future generations could live in a peaceful democratic country on the other side of the world should inspire us to make sure that we value the freedoms we have. The history included gives a very brief look at a society that little has been heard of. For further information read the history books listed.

To offer this technique, I needed to make another journey of discovery in a very different direction. This time it was to learn how to better use my Apple Mac computer to enable me to prepare clear instructions. Because the stitches are not all worked over a four thread count and a number of them are not included in western embroidery books, colour-coded graphs for each of the patterns, tacking diagrams, pattern layouts and stitch diagrams were needed. These useful aids make working the unfamiliar patterns that change the thread count regularly simpler to work and they are also excellent for pattern placement. The tacking and colour-coded graphs also ensure that as each pattern block is worked the thread count is correct and there will not be an unpleasant surprise when the patterns do not meet around the cloth. Some of the patterns have been developed from the 'D.M.C. Openwork' booklet, others have been created from various portions of work seen in photographs of museum pieces and illustrations in books published in Ukraine. My aim has been to keep the patterns included true to what is known in Ukraine.

Ukrainian Whitework is a luxuriant, rich, heritage needlework technique, ideal for those special projects that could become family heirlooms. As well as for decorative domestic linen the many splendid borders and bands of rich stitching make wonderful band samplers and two of the borders have been used locally for altar cloths. The patterns or portions of them are also ideal for small very acceptable gift items, i.e., lavender bags, bookmarks and needlebooks. Ukrainian Whitework is an excellent follow-on for those who enjoy traditional embroidery techniques and are looking for a new challenge.

I trust that you will gain as much pleasure from this technique as I have.

Gaynor M. Eaton, Dunedin, New Zealand 2004

History — Ukraine

The early history of Ukraine is lost in the mists of the distant past. The Greek historian Herodotus writing in the mid 5th century B.C. gives a graphic account of his travels in Ukraine and the funeral ceremonies conducted by the Scythian people for their dead kings. Recent archaeological investigation of their huge burial mounds corroborates much of his writing; the masterpieces of goldsmithing found clearly illustrate the artistic skill and craftsmanship of these ancient people.[1]

Information about the settlement of Slavic peoples in present day Ukraine is found chiefly in the records of Arabic and Greek travellers and merchants of the day. During the middle centuries of the first millennium A.D. they spread outwards from a fairly confined territory somewhere in east-central Europe; over time they split into three main branches, Western, Southern and Eastern. The Eastern Slavs include Ukrainians, Belarussians and Russians. The Slavic expansion is poorly documented. Evidently it did not have the suddenness or military character that would have alarmed and threatened the Romans and Byzantines[2].

Ukraine was known as Kyivian Rus from the ninth century A.D. until its destruction in the thirteenth century by the Tartars. From the mid ninth century the Vikings were very active in the region travelling down the rivers from the Baltic to the Black Sea and into the Mediterranean to trade and raid, and so became involved with Kyiv (Kiev) on the Dnieper River, a great centre owing its riches to trade with the Byzantium Empire.[3] Christianity became the state religion of Kyivian Rus in 988 when Prince Volodymyr of Kyiv converted to the Byzantium Greek Orthodox faith. The Primary Chronicle (or more literally, The Tales of Bygone Years) describes a mass baptism in the Dnieper River of the people of Kyiv which followed.[4] "The mission arose in Constantinople (Istanbul) and was confirmed and supported by Pope Adrian II and his successors. If Slavic Christianity was conceived as Orthodoxy in union with Rome with the Pope as the Head of the Church, then it is in Ukraine that this ideal has never died and remains the same today."[5] "The Eastern rite established by the time of the Byzantine Emperor Justinian the Great (483–565) still continues to this day that allows that only celibates could be bishops, while clergy below that rank could marry before ordination."[6,7] "Today the majority in the East are Ukrainian Orthodox, the west are mostly Ukrainian Catholics of the Eastern Byzantine rite, a small very active group are Baptists."[8]

Ukrainians' conversion to Christianity opened new fields for the spread of Byzantine art. It is the miracle of Byzantine art that without a break it could become the art of the Slav peoples and must be attributed to the Greek Orthodox Church of Constantinople and the prestige of that city which epitomised civilisation throughout the Middle Ages.[9] In Kyiv a church of St. Sofia

[1] Scythians, a nomadic people of Iranian stock, migrated from Central Asia to Ukraine 8th–7th B.C. and centred on what is now known as the Crimea. *Encyclopaedia Britannica* 2002

[2] Robin Milner-Gulland with Nikolai Dejevsky (1989). *Atlas of Russia and the Soviet Union.* Phaidon.

[3] Graham-Campbell, James, & Kidd, Dafydd (1980). *The Vikings.* British Museum Publications.

[4] Pavlyshyn, Marko (Ed.). (1988). *One Thousand Years of Christianity in Ukraine.* Monash University.

[5] *op cit.*

[6] Walker, W., Norris, R., Lotz, A., Handy, D. W., & Robert, P. (1986). *A History of the Christian Church.* T & T Clark Ltd, Edinburgh. 4th edition.

[7] Read Stephan's story, page 91.

[8] Kardash, Peter. (1991). *Ukraine Its History and Its Arts.* Fortuna Co., Melbourne.

[9] Lassus, Jean. (1976). *The Early Christian & Byzantine World.* Hamlyn.

was founded about 1027; it was a metropolitan cathedral intended to play the same role as the Hagia Sofia in Constantinople. Over the last ten centuries St. Sofia has undergone many changes, but has always been, and remains for every Ukrainian, the symbolic and religious embodiment of Ukrainian faith, culture and statehood, even though in 1934 the Soviet authorities forcibly closed the cathedral and confiscated all objects of value. The structure has now been converted into the Sophijskyi museum and architectural memorial. Though all churches were destroyed prior to the outbreak of World War II, "Christianity survived because believers secretly worshipped in their homes."[10]

"Ukraine is literally translated as 'borderland' and that is exactly what it is, flat, fertile and fatally tempting to invaders. It is on the crossroads between Europe, Asia and the Middle East and has been the buffer and the bulwark of European civilisation. It has been constantly subjugated by its enemies who have exploited its natural and human resources for their own benefit to the detriment of its people."[11] Over the centuries it has been overrun by Vikings, Tartars and Mongols, its boundary continually changed as Russia, Poland, Austria, Czechoslovakia, Romania and Germany used it as a brutally savage battlefield. In the early 1400s Cossack outposts were established to protect their land and peoples. From about 1654 Ukraine eventually came under Russian domination in spite of the courageous efforts of the Cossacks to remain as a sovereign nation. Farmers came under the Russian system of serfdom. Though theoretically free tenants, they were exploited by the lords who demanded ever larger shares of the crops, animals, labour and this put them in steadily mounting debt.[12] By the end of the 17th century their status scarcely differed from that of chattel slaves. The French Revolution of 1789 virtually eliminated serfdom throughout western Europe. In eastern Europe, however, and particularly in Russia, the system persisted until it was finally abolished in 1861 by Tsar Alexander II.[13]

"In 1863 an edict declared that there was no Ukrainian language, merely a dialect of Russian."[14] Books that were educational, religious and for schools were banned and newspapers closed down. Then in 1876 Czar Alexander II issued a proclamation prohibiting the publication of all books and material in the Ukrainian language except for historical documents. Ukrainian theatre and musical performances were forbidden. One Ukrainian word uttered unguardedly in public was branded as nationalism, which the authorities interpreted as fascism, and that called for the mandatory ten years' penalty working in Siberian salt mines. The greater the value of the victim to the community the harsher and longer the punishment. "Throughout this difficult period the national idea was preserved by poets and intellectuals and in 1897 a General Ukrainian Democratic Organization was illegally founded to co-ordinate their cultural and social groups."[15]

The Russian revolution of 1917 gave Ukrainians hope of independence, but that only lasted until 1922 when the long bloody and oppressive occupation by Bolshevik Russia began. "Between 1929 and 1932 the Soviet Communist Party struck a double blow at Ukrainian people: *dekulakization*, the dispossession and deportation of millions of farming families and collectivization, the effective abolition of private property in land and the concentration of the remaining farmers in 'collective' farms under party control. This was followed in 1932–33 by a 'terror-famine' which the State inflicted on the collectivized farmers of

[10] Kardash, Peter. (1991). *Ukraine Its History and Its Arts*. Fortuna Co., Melbourne.

[11] Senator Pav Yuzyk (2002), Professor of History University of Ottawa, Canada. 'Ukraine in World History'.

[12] Reid, Anna. (1997). *Borderland*. Weidenfeld & Nicolson, London.

[13] Conquest, Robert. (1986). *The Harvest of Sorrow* . Oxford University Press.

[14] *op cit.*

[15] *op cit.*

Ukraine by setting impossibly high grain quotas, removing every other source food and preventing help from outside."[16] The authorities sent in 120 000 military police to remove every other source of food. Approximately 7–10 million died as the result of these actions, many more than the total number of deaths for all the countries in the First World War.[17] Ukraine was a battlefield for most of the Second World War. The Nazi invasion of 1941 brought death to another six million Ukrainians. Just as during the "terror-famine" of 1932–33 many had to sell their embroidery and other possessions to buy or exchange for food, e.g, it is recorded that a richly embroidered tablecloth had been exchanged for a 4 lb loaf of bread.[18] On 26 April 1986 at 1.23 A.M. the Chornobyl nuclear tragedy occurred. Many lost their lives, over 100 000 were evacuated, and the city of Prypyat remains deserted to this day.[19]

The Ukrainian people were eventually freed from Soviet Russia's domination when they won independence as a democratic state on 24 August 1991. But the battle is not over. Ukraine has inherited the effects of mismanagement and the ruination of its culture, language and traditions. Until very recently Ukraine's neighbours did not see it as a separate country or Ukrainians as a separate people, and refused to acknowledge the existence of such a thing as "Ukrainian" history. To Russians it was part of Russia; to Poles part of Poland, and many Ukrainians Russified or Polonised by centuries of foreign domination thought the same way.[20]

Ukraine lies in the southern part of Eastern Europe and borders the Black Sea, Romania, Hungary, Czechoslovakia, Poland, Belarus and Russia, and is the second largest country in Europe with a population of 49.5 million (2002). Its capital city is Kyiv which is one of the oldest and most historic towns of the old U.S.S.R. Ukraine is the richest agricultural region in Europe and is known as the 'Bread Basket of Europe'. It is also rich in natural resources and an important industrial power that is amongst Europe's largest producers of coal, iron ore, steel, manganese and chemicals.

The Crimea war 1854–56 brought Ukraine (then part of Russia) into the news of the day. It is perhaps better remembered now for the contribution and superhuman efforts of Florence Nightingale. She revolutionised the treatment and care of the soldiers, she was made a national heroine by the British army and public, and went on to establish sound nursing practices.

Many Ukrainians have immigrated to Western European countries, Canada, U.K., U.S.A. and South America. At the end of the Second World War approximately 21 000 settled in Australia from the displaced persons' camps in West Germany.[21] For the first two years they worked as directed and since then have established themselves as valued citizens of that country. They have provided opportunities for their young people to learn about their rich cultural heritage and have given funds to establish lectureships in the Ukrainian language at both Monash and Macquarie Universities. They have established villages for their elderly, built seventeen Ukrainian Orthodox and seventeen Ukrainian Catholic churches. Beside the Ukrainian Catholic Cathedral of Melbourne they have built a museum to house their extensive, comprehensive collection of Arts and Crafts. Other museums have been established in Adelaide and Canberra, Australia. The Ukrainian Women's Association of Australia has a wide range of aims and objectives that include retaining and promoting Ukrainian

---

[16] Conquest, Robert. (1986). *The Harvest of Sorrow* . Oxford University Press.
[17] Kardash, Peter. (1991). *Ukraine Its History and Its Arts*. Fortuna Co., Melbourne.
[18] Conquest, Robert. (1986). *The Harvest of Sorrow* . Oxford University Press.
[19] Kardash, Peter. (1991). *Ukraine Its History and Its Arts*. Fortuna Co., Melbourne.
[20] Reid, Anna. (1997). *Borderland.* Weidenfeld & Nicolson, London.
[21] Pavlyshyn, Marko (Ed.). (1986). *Ukrainian Settlement in Australia.* Monash University.

culture and traditions, community work, support for the elderly, sponsorship of underprivileged children, plus many more.

Taras Shevchenko (1814–61), a descendant of serfdom, is the force that united the well educated and the ordinary people and inspired in them a love for Ukraine by his poetry and art.[22] Robert Conquest states that "his influence cannot be exaggerated."[23] He suffered greatly under the tsars and was sentenced to 25 years' penal service in the Russian army which was forcing the tsarist regime onto the indigenous people of Central Asia. Shevchenko was an artist of international standing, a poet, a prophet, a mental giant. His 'Kobzar', book of poetry is found in almost every Ukrainian home. He was the Moses of the Ukrainian people who led them out of the wilderness. His poem *I Care Not* still speaks to us today from the very soul of Ukraine.

I CARE NOT
Taras Shevchenko (1814–61)

I care not, shall I see my dear
Own land before I die, or no,
Nor who forgets me, buried here
In desert wastes of alien snow;
Though all forget me — better so

A slave from my first bitter years,
Most surely I shall die a slave
Ungraced of any kinsmen's tears
And carry with me to my grave

Everything; and leave no trace,
No little mark to keep my place
In the dear lost Ukraine
Which is not ours, though our land.
And none shall ever understand;
No father to his son shall say:
kneel down and fold your hands, and pray;
He died for our Ukraine.

I care no longer if the child
Shall pray for me, or pass me by.
One only thing I cannot bear:
To know my land, that was beguiled
Into a death-trap with a lie,
Trampled and ruined and defiled.
Ah, but I care, dear God; I care!

[22] Kardash, Peter. (1991). *Ukraine Its History and Its Arts*. Fortuna Co., Melbourne.
[23] Conquest, Robert. (1986). *The Harvest of Sorrow* . Oxford University Press.

History — Ukrainian Embroidery

One of the earliest surviving pieces of needlework from Ukraine is a quilted funerary carpet discovered by the Koslov expedition of 1924–25. It is now in the Leningrad Department of the Institute of Archaeology of the Academy of Sciences, and thought to have been made during the first century B.C. by the Scythian people.[1] The technical skill and artistry of this work clearly shows a long cultural tradition that must have stretched back well into the mists of time. It is evident from writings of fifth century wandering Arabs, and chronicles written when the Ukrainian people accepted Christianity, that clear reference was made to the embroidered clothing worn.[2]

Ornamental embroidery had been widespread in Ukraine long before the adoption of Christianity and was linked with ancient protective symbols and folk traditions. The introduction of Christianity in the 10th century gave rise to ecclesiastical embroidery, which like icon painting, was to serve the church well. Embroidery workshops were established to produce images of saints and religious subjects that adorned ecclesiastical vestments as well as various icon cloths, hangings and palls. Like icons, these embroideries were an important part of religious ceremonies. The ability of both designers and embroiderers is seen in the exquisitely executed works of art that continued in the Byzantium tradition. Magnificent examples of this work can be seen at The Victoria and Albert Museum, London, including one dated 1407.[3] The Zagorsk Museum collection provides a vivid idea of the ecclesiastical and ornamental embroidery of the 15–17th centuries.[4] Some of the pieces illustrated in that catalogue show motifs and techniques seen in their domestic embroidery.

"Embroideries were the product of local cultures fused together with the cultures of all nations that had conquered and settled or had passed through the area."[5] "The advent of Christianity and its acceptance was the first great unifying force throughout the region. Constantinople (Istanbul), the New Rome, became the centre of a Christian empire within which all its races and religions lived a fairly harmonious life sharing a common culture."[6] Ukraine came under the influence of the Byzantium empire early, and eventually adopted the Byzantine way of worship which they have held onto to this day. "The art of embroidery developed many centuries ago was of utmost importance in the lives of Ukrainian people."[7] During the 18th and 19th centuries highly skilled embroiderers created matchless masterpieces of clothing and furnishings that were richly decorated in a wide variety of stitches and patterns. The embroidery on the sleeves of women's shirts was the richest, and harmonised with the other garments worn. The location of a decoration and the character of a pattern as well as its colour depended upon local traditions and the style of the garment. Provinces, regions and even villages had their own specific type of folk costume which was a real work of art. Many motifs are named figuratively: "sheep horns", "windmill", "ox eye", etc. Each composition has a great number of variants depending upon the combination of their forms and general selection of the colours. Many used splendid floral patterns with roses, poppies and pinks;

[1] Colby, Averil. (1972). *Quilting.* Batsford.

[2] Kutsenko, Maria. (1977). *Ukrainian Embroideries.* Spectrum Publications, Melbourne.

[3] Synge, Lanto. (2001). *Art of Embroidery—History of Style and Technique.* Antique Collectors' Club.

[4] *Early Russian Embroidery in the Zagorsk Museum Collection.* (1983).

[5] Taylor, Roderick. (1998). *Embroidery of the Greek Islands and Epirus.* Marston House

[6] Taylor, Roderick. (1993). *Ottoman Embroidery.* Marston House.

[7] Paine, Sheila (1990). *Embroidered Textiles, Traditional Patterns from Five Continents.* Thames & Hudson.

others chose geometric patterns with kloster blocks, eyelets, stitched braids and drawn thread work, all densely stitched.[8]

Every farmer and villager grew flax and hemp for their seeds, a valuable source of oil. Flax fibre was used for the production of fine textiles for domestic use; hemp fibre was utilised for sacking and rope making. Village women met together to stitch, spin, gossip and sing their beautiful folk songs. Children from the age of five were taught embroidery along with spinning and weaving. In accordance with ancient customs wives and daughters in farming families were obliged to provide the family with all the necessary clothing and household linens.

There are over 100 stitches in Ukrainian needlework; some are familiar friends that can be found in a Mary Thomas stitch dictionary; others are unknown in the west. At the beginning of the 19th century cross stitch was introduced, and because of its simplicity, it soon became so popular that many of the more complicated stitches previously used became outdated and forgotten. Olena Kulynych-Stakhurska writes that: "there are now unfortunately few places where Ukrainian embroidery continues to exist. Our people long for art but because of the absence of authentic pattern-making, fancywork is incredibly extemporised." She urges her readers to keep their rich traditions alive and restore them to their former worth.[9] Tania Diakiw O'Neill has a very similar message for her readers. She states that: "the wealth of Ukrainian embroidery design stems largely from the variety of stitching techniques used throughout Ukraine. Unfortunately, the knowledge and use of many of these techniques is dying out, and cross stitch has displaced the more ancient and lovelier stitches."[10]

Ukrainian Whitework is a little known technique that comes mainly from around Poltava, east Ukraine, an old city on a trade route between the Baltic, Black Sea and Greece. In 1708 it was the battleground where Peter the Great of Russia routed Charles XII of Sweden. A little whitework is also found in Podollia, west Ukraine. Ukrainian Whitework features cut kloster blocks, pulled fabric eyelets, geometric satin stitch and drawn thread borders. The only two Western European books found that include Ukrainian Whitework are the *D.M.C. Encyclopedia of Needlework*[11] and their booklet *Openwork Embroidery*.[12] It was the photographs of the rich borders in that booklet that provided the inspiration and original information for this book.

Norway's hardanger is similar to Ukrainian Whitework as both styles include kloster blocks. However the Ukrainian method of working kloster blocks is quite different, they are often over a three thread count and a cross stitch is worked at each corner before the bars are overcast.[13] Maria Kutsenko states that there is a firm foundation for believing that the method of working kloster blocks came from the Byzantium and that the Greek method of working them is identical to Ukraine's.[14] Lefkara whitework of Cyprus is similar to Ukrainian Whitework with its deep richly worked borders that include satin stitch motifs, cut work and drawn thread borders.[15] It, too, came under the influence of the Byzantium empire.

[8] Klimova, Nina T. (1981). *Folk Embroidery of the USSR.* Van Nostrand Reinhold Co., U.S.A.

[9] Kulynych-Stakhurska, Olena. (1996). *The Art of Ukrainian Embroidery Techniques and Technology, Lviv.*

[10] Diakiw O'Neill, Tania. (2000). *Ukrainian Embroidery Techniques.* STO Publications, U.S.A. 2nd ed.

[11] De Dillmont, Therese. (1971). *Encyclopedia of Needlework.* De Dillmont, France.

[12] De Dillmont, Therese, S.à.r.l. (1930s?), *Openwork Embroidery* D.M.C. Library, Mulhouse, France.

[13] Diakiw O'Neill, Tania. (2000). *Ukrainian Embroidery Techniques.* STO Publications, U.S.A. 2nd ed.

[14] Kutsenko, Maria. (1977). *Ukrainian Embroideries.* Spectrum Publications, Melbourne.

[15] Hadjiyiasemi, Androula. (1987). *Lefkara lace embroidery.* Proodos Printing & Publishing Co., Nicosia Cyprus

One of the features that makes Ukrainian whitework different, and not found in any of the well known stitch dictionaries, is the pulled fabric round eyelets that link together either in rows or blocks. In Ukraine they are known as nightingale eyes and provide a lovely textural contrast to the smooth satin stitch. There is reference to them in *Folk Embroidery of the USSR*[16] and the D.M.C. *Openwork Embroidery*.[17] To work eyelets on the closely woven linen of the past both a warp and a weft thread had to be cut, the hole was widened with a stiletto and then bound firmly with close stitching. Another different feature is the way that the satin stitch fillings are sometimes broken up into smaller blocks to give a shorter stitch length, but more importantly to give a broken texture or crenellated edge that catches the light beautifully. This method of working was seen on a detail of a 17th century purificator and is used for the Stephan, Olya and Sofia patterns.

Many of the rich, deep borders are edged with a band of drawn thread needle weaving or wrapping. These drawn thread borders, irrespective of size or style, are known as merezhka. They are further embellished with a row of small motifs worked at the outer edges. Unlike West European counted thread work, most of the patterns are not worked over the same thread count. It may be either a three and four or, two and three and even a two, three and four count. When turning a corner this does sometimes require a "fudge point". Originally Ukrainian Whitework was worked on hand spun and woven linen that was not even weave, and was generally worked as a straight band on clothing and not usually as a four-sided border that required a turned corner and an accurate thread count.

I am indebted to Orion Wenhrynowycz and Michael (Mychajlo) Hanytsky of Melbourne for their keen interest and unstinting valuable help in sourcing information and stories to include in this book. They escaped West Ukraine ahead of the retreating German army. In 1947 they were in a West German displaced persons' camp and took the Australian government's offer to settle in that country. These two gentlemen have been curators of the Ukrainian Arts and Crafts Museum, Melbourne, and are passionate about keeping their culture alive on the other side of the world. When I visited the Ukrainian Arts and Crafts Museum they generously gave their time to show examples of Ukrainian Whitework. They also sent to my home in New Zealand books and photographs of original work that I have been able to adapt for today's needlework. Like them, I too believe it would be a great pity if this stunningly beautiful heritage technique became a lost treasure.

Australian Museum Collections

The Ukrainian Arts and Crafts Museum, 35 Canning Street, North Melbourne, Victoria 3051.

The Ukrainian Museum, 6 George St, Hindmarsh, SA 5007, Adelaide.

Ukrainian Orthodox Centre Canberra, Millennium Memorial Museum, 6 McKay Gardens, Turner, ACT 2612.

---

[16] Klimova, Nina T. (1981). *Folk Embroidery of the USSR*. Van Nostrand Reinhold Co., U.S.A.

[17] De Dillmont, Therese, S.à.r.l. (1930s?), *Openwork Embroidery* D.M.C. Library, Mulhouse, France.

Ukrainian Whitework

The introduction to this technique came from the D.M.C. Library *Openwork Embroidery*, published by TH. DE Dillmont, S.à.r.l. Mulhouse, France. My copy is undated and was given to me by the late Miss Helen M. Moran.[1] She had used this booklet during her years of teaching needlework in Dunedin and had given it to me when I began teaching. I am most grateful to DMC for allowing me to include a pattern from their booklet, that I have named Maria. It was not until I had spoken with Michael Hanytsky and Orion Wenhrynowycz at the Ukrainian Arts and Crafts Museum, Melbourne, that I knew for sure what the technique was.

The patterns illustrated in *Openwork Embroidery* are straight borders used on clothing. In the past these borders would have been worked on hand spun and woven linen that were not evenweave and because the border was straight the thread count did not need to be accurate. Most examples of Ukrainian Whitework feature kloster blocks. As they are so well known I have chosen instead to include only patterns that feature eyelets. Round eyelets would seem to be unique to Ukrainian embroidery, they vary in size, are a pulled fabric technique and worked on the diagonal, sometimes in groups and often used to outline the shape. As well there are also square and buttonhole eyelets. Some of the patterns also feature both of the pulled fabric faggot stitches; they and the eyelets work very well together.

To provide further examples I have adapted, developed and designed patterns from photographs of museum pieces and needlework books published in Ukraine and from the examples illustrated in 'Openwork Embroidery'. Though these patterns are different from the original they are still recognisable as Ukrainian Whitework. The books published in Ukraine illustrated that many of the satin stitch motifs had crenellated edges instead of the smooth edge seen in West European needlework. As can be seen I have used this style of satin stitch frequently; it catches the light beautifully and adds further interest to the work. Another useful option found to work with satin stitch is the double running filling stitch; it breaks up the length of a stitch and provides extra texture. The Anna, Iryna and Olya patterns were designed to provide patterns that included the large round eyelets. The Olya pattern also gives another method of Ukrainian Whitework pattern making where the motif changes direction sharply.

The patterns with the square eyelets were designed from photographs of their traditional white work shirts worn on festive occasions. These shirts have bands of rich stitching worked around the upper sleeves. The linen used was closely woven, similar to the linens used for cutwork and not suitable for counted thread work (see page 78). It has been a fascinating challenge to design these patterns to be recognizable as Ukrainian Whitework. Other techniques included are pattern darning and drawn thread.

To complete the rich embellishment and stylish symphony of pattern and stitch the borders are edged with bands of needle weaving, wrapping or layering. All drawn thread work in Ukraine is known as Merezhka from the simplest border to the most complex. They are then finished with narrow borders of satin stitch or motifs of eyelets or bands of verkhoploot top winding. It is this combination of rich satin stitch, textural pulled fabric stitches and various

---

[1] Miss Moran was brought to Dunedin, New Zealand from the U.K. in 1929 by the King Edward Technical College to teach needlework to their day, evening and tertiary students. Her influence was remarkable and is a major factor in the strength and interest that there is today in embroidery throughout this country. See *Southern People* 1998 published by the Dunedin City Council.

styles of drawn thread work that makes Ukrainian whitework distinctively different from other traditional techniques.

Ukrainian Whitework is not just worked over the usual four × four threads. The patterns can be over both three × three and four × four threads and a few are over two × two, three × three and four × four threads. This can create a problem at the corners, dealt with by working one stitch over an extra thread count. This "fudge" point is marked on the pattern graph. This thread count change is another special feature of Ukrainian Whitework and gives it a distinctive charm and beauty. Many of the stitches and methods of working are not included in our well known stitch dictionaries and bring to West European work valuable additions to our stitch vocabulary.

Each of the patterns is named for a Ukrainian and gives something of that person's story. Iryna and Olena live in New Zealand. The other patterns are named for Ukrainians living in Australia or for their parents or relatives in Ukraine.

The pieces illustrated are worked on either 25, 28 or 30 count linens with perle, stranded and sewing cottons. Because fabric threads are only cut for the drawn thread borders, more open linens could be chosen if eyesight is a problem.

Work a Practice Sampler
To practise the patterns and needlewoven borders keep a sampler in your work basket to try the different patterns and stitches before beginning a masterpiece. If using linen or evenweave fabric other than what is suggested it is always worthwhile to check that the fabric threads will darn back into the cloth easily and without showing. These samplers become valuable, useful reference material for future projects.

Embroidery is deeply entrenched in almost all aspects of everyday life in a Ukrainian village family. Here the folklore, customs and rituals survived the longest and outlived the Soviet era. They are now undergoing a spontaneous revival. When Anna was being courted she followed the ancient traditions handed down through the centuries and embroidered two oblong pieces of ritual cloth known as 'rushnyk'. The ancient custom was for the young man courting a girl with the intention of marrying her to send two matchmakers to negotiate the marriage proposal and dowry with her parents. When the matchmakers arrived at Anna's home they knew that they were successful when she tied the rushnyk cloths that she had embroidered diagonally across their shoulders. The wedding preparations went ahead and they all enjoyed a sumptuous meal prepared by Anna and her family.

Requirements

Linen

Good quality linen has been used for all the examples shown. The Kateryna, Michael, Orion, Sofia and Stephan patterns plus the pattern darning table mats are all worked on linens purchased many years ago. Excellent alternative brands than those given are available in specialist needlework shops. For drawn thread work it is preferable to use linen that has a well spun round thread that withdraws readily without shredding and breaking, i.e., Dublin, Permin and Semco.

If eyesight is a problem select a linen that you can comfortably count the threads. Calculate the extra required from the number of threads that the pattern requires or apply percentages. From a 30 count to a 25 count add 20%. A 30 count to a 20 count add 50%. A 25 count to a 20 count add 25%.

Semco is the brand name for the Belgium linen sold in New Zealand and Australia. It is marketed under other brands elsewhere.

Selvedges: Cut wide selvedge edges off and machine neaten the raw edges. For the narrow selvedge edges of the older types of linen like Lauder and Glenshee, withdraw approximately three threads at the edge to ease the weave.

To neaten and secure cut edges of table linen:

To ensure that the linen is cut straight, withdraw a thread and cut on that line. Secure the cut raw edges by oversewing by hand or with machine stitching. For machine stitching use matching cottons and the multiple serpentine machine stitch as shown, keep the length short and width to cover the 5–6 threads at the cut fabric edge. Let the machine feed the fabric through without pulling and distorting the stitching. This machine stitching remains in place, hidden under the hem and keeps the weave secure.

I prefer machine stitching, it has kept the raw edges of my evenweave linen teaching samplers secure for twenty five years. This was good advice given by the late Miss Helen M. Moran from her long years of teaching.

To neaten and secure cut edges of small projects:

As a general rule for most small projects, withdraw two threads on the four sides to the finished size required. It is important to remember that the extra linen is cut off only after the edge has been completed. This keeps the linen flat and avoids the edge from frilling. For bookmarks the edging needs to be stitched around the four sides to keep the top of the fringe secure.

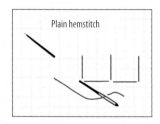

Plain hemstitch

Option 1. For an unlined bookmark or similar. Machine serpentine stitch the edge as above. Have the stitch width set to cover just the 3–4 linen threads at the edge and use the two withdrawn threads as a guide to keep the machining straight. This serpentine stitched edge can then be covered by working buttonhole stitch over it, between every thread and across four threads.

Option 2. To cover the six linen threads at the edge of the piece, work two rows of plain hemstitch each over 3 × 3 threads and with the straight stitch away from the edge and the extra linen that will be cut off. This edge stitching should be firm as it is what will hold the linen from fraying.

Option 3. For a lined bookmark. Withdraw the two threads to mark the finished size. Cut a fine cotton lining a little larger than required; bond it onto the reverse side of the embroidery with bond-a-web or similar. Buttonhole around the four sides, through both fabrics over 4 threads and between each. Once completed carefully cut both fabrics away from the edge.

Threads: Select a quality thread that is colour fast.

- Perle 8 for satin stitch, looped hemstitch, merezhka Poltavska, pattern darning, verkhoploot borders and needle weaving.

- Perle 12 for eyelets, the faggot stitches, zig zag buttonhole borders, needle wrapped borders, hemstitch and woven corner fillings.

- Perle 12 has a limited colour range and is not always available. The alternatives that I have found to work well are Coats Duet sewing cotton. It is a cotton covered polyester machine thread, there is a wide range of colours and it can be used both single or double, see the Anna and Olya patterns. Other substitutes for perle 12 are No. 60–80 mercerised crochet cotton, bobbin lace making threads, topstitching or quilting cottons. Test first to ensure that the alternative thread is suitable, does not twist and knot and is colour fast.

- Stranded cotton, 2 strands may be used for square and buttonhole eyelets, drawn thread zig zag buttonhole borders, needle wrapped borders and hemstitch.

- To ensure the same colour batch purchase enough thread to complete the project. For a 100 cm square cloth with a needle woven border approximately 4–6 balls of No. 8 perle cotton and 2 to 3 balls of No. 12 perle.

- For satin stitch, to give good cover the working thread should be slightly thicker than the fabric threads. Select perle cotton No. 8 for 25–30 count fabrics and No. 5 perle for 20 count fabrics.

- For pulled fabric, because the fabric weave will be under tension a round fine, strong thread is required to give the lacy effect. Select perle 12, or one of the alternatives listed above.

- To hem with matching thread, use threads withdrawn from the weave of the linen, short lengths only. If they are a soft spun keep twisting them while working. This is a good option when not wanting to emphasise the hemstitch line.

- Test for colour fastness if using a new or unfamiliar thread.

- If threads knot, try threading the needle from the opposite end.

- To loosen a knot, prise it apart with two needles.

Starting threads:

- To begin stitching hold approximately 5–6 cm of thread in place with a back stitch on the front of the work and out of the way of the stitching.

- When working the small round eyelets and other closely worked stitches hold approximately 5–6 cm of the thread tail in place on the underside and make sure that the stitching covers it for its full length.

- When using a thread double i.e. stranded or sewing cotton, thread the needle with the two cut ends and as the first stitch is made take the needle through the end loop to secure it.

- Bring in a new thread before finishing off the old one and weave it into place to work the next stitch. Once further stitches have been worked finish the old thread off neatly in the back of the work. This method ensures that the stitching can continue without losing the place or a break showing in the stitching.

Finish threads off neatly and securely as you work rather than leave them until the embroidery is completed.

- For pulled work, because the thread is under tension take one or two back stitches as you carry 5–6 cm of the thread under them.

- For satin stitch slide the thread under the back of the work without making any back stitches that would distort the smooth surface.
- Drawn thread corner borders. There will be at least two lengths of No. 8 perle cotton to finish off. Darn each of them into the new selvedge edge to be hidden under the buttonhole stitch that will be worked over it, then carry them up through the needle woven tubes at the corner to strengthen and support the woven corner filling.
- The No. 12 perle left from the hemstitching can be used to work buttonhole stitch over the new selvedge edge and to work the woven corner filling.

Tools:

- Small round frame, bind the inner ring with either white or cream bias binding or cotton tape. The linen should be held firmly in the frame and removed when not working.
- Tapestry needles, the eye to be large enough to carry thread without bruising it.
- Crewel needles are used to finish off the working thread in the back of firmly pulled fabric work.
- Small sharp pointed scissors.
- A sampler to try out the various stitches and patterns is a very useful item to include in the work basket.
- Stilettos were traditionally used to open the weave of the linen when working eyelets.
- Good light is essential. A lamp positioned at the back of the chair is a worthwhile addition to the needle worker's equipment.

Unpicking:

Every good needlewoman unpicks work that is unsatisfactory.

- Before cutting a thread lift it with the head of the needle to avoid cutting the linen.
- To settle the weave back into place again, scratch its back while held taut in a frame.
- Unpicked threads should be discarded; if reused they may spoil the work.

Small pieces of linen, i.e., bookmarks, needlebooks and lavender bags. If the linen is too small to hold firmly in the frame, extend the size by sewing strips of calico or similar along each side. Or place the linen over a larger piece of calico and machine around the outer edge with a large stitch, then cut the calico away from the underside to allow stitching.

Name and date your work in the hem with a simple back stitch. The name should be in full, not just initials. Ukrainian Whitework is heritage needlework that will become a treasured family heirloom. Within just a few years initials do not clearly state whose good work it is. This information could include the date begun and finished and if it was made as a gift for a special occasion or any other relevant information.

Tacking

"Today's preparation determines tomorrow's achievement"

Preparation:

- Tacking charts and colour coded graphs are included with each pattern.
- A tacked grid is a useful method for pattern placement. It also ensures that by following it, the embroidery count is accurate and the pattern will meet around the four sides when completed.
- Use bright, fast colour sewing cotton that is easily seen.
- Colour code tacking for centre, length, width and hems.
- All tacking to be accurate, if not find and fix. If the miscount is hard to find turn the work over, it may show up on the underside.
- The first two tacking lines divide the linen into four portions.
- Fold the linen or measure it to find the half, then tack over and under from edge to edge the thread count the pattern requires.
- Start the second length of tacking at the cloth centre, it does not cross over the first length but meets in the same space and at a 90° angle.
- Once the tacking has divided the linen into four sections follow the tacking grids given with each pattern.
- The tacking lines extend out to each side of the cloth as shown and mark the start and finish of each pattern unit.
- Do not remove the tacking until the cloth is completed. It is used for placing small motifs and narrow borders at the edge of the main pattern.
- The tacking is shown as fine black lines drawn on each graphed pattern.

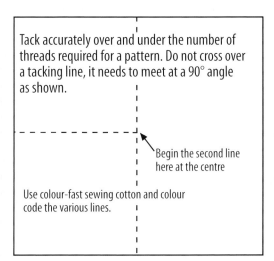

Tack accurately over and under the number of threads required for a pattern. Do not cross over a tacking line, it needs to meet at a 90° angle as shown.

Begin the second line here at the centre

Use colour-fast sewing cotton and colour code the various lines.

To find where to place a pattern:

Start at the cloth centre, mark each pattern width, not depth with tacking on the centre lines. The tacking diagrams and pattern layouts are given with each pattern.

- For a border to fit it may need to be placed across the centre tacking or begun there to give either an even or uneven number of pattern blocks. Note the Iryna pattern requires an even number of pattern blocks.

- Once where the pattern will be worked has been found, tack both the upper and lower edges and the centre lines as drawn on the pattern graphs, but not shown on the tacking diagrams.
- At the outer edge allow a further 50–120 threads for the drawn thread, narrow borders, small motifs and hem. This depends upon the requirements and the space available.
- For a runner tack the centre as above then the number of pattern blocks along the centre line and both edges of the pattern.
- Tack the hemstitching lines, see hems page 111.
- As a useful guide mark the centre of the cloth and the right side of the linen with a secure tailor's tack.

When working a corner:

- It is useful to tack a diagonal line into the corner, keep it to the same thread count and placement as the rest of the tacking.
- To stitch the corner, use two needles and threads, one from each side of the pattern and work towards the tacked corner where the stitching will meet.
- This useful method is used for the Sofia pattern, where the motifs meet at the inner corner.

To find where to turn a corner:

If turning at a place other than shown on the photograph and graphed pattern use the well tested method of placing a mirror over a border to find a pleasing place to turn. Work a portion of the border on a practice sampler, make two photocopies of it then either cut or fold them and place as seen in the mirror.

Stitches are the vocabulary of needlework and are used to describe the various lines, textures, patterns and motifs. The diagrams are colour coded when a return row is included. To achieve the best result and before beginning a project, it is always worthwhile to practise stitches and patterns on a sampler with various weights and types of thread. The dotted lines show where the needle travels on the underside, the arrows where it enters the cloth.

Reverse faggot is a pulled fabric stitch; it can either be worked as a single row as shown, or double to give a stronger line. The needles are placed to show the method of changing direction. The stitch is seen on the front of the work as a diagonal line and features in many of the patterns. It is usually worked with No. 12 perle cotton or similar.

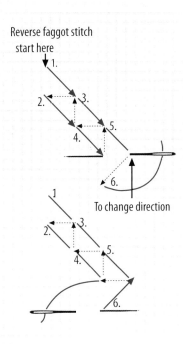

Reverse faggot stitch
start here

To change direction

Single faggot is another pulled fabric stitch that is usually worked with No. 12 perle cotton or similar. It is generally worked in two rows to give a diagonal line of boxes. Each row is a series of back stitches that are straight on the right side, however on the wrong side it is the same as reverse faggot with the stitches on the diagonal.

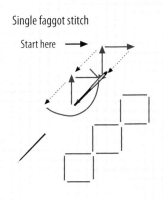

Single faggot stitch

Start here →

Double running filling stitch is an ideal method of breaking up long satin stitches and adding texture where the thread enters the linen within a wide block. The arrows show the needle and thread movements.

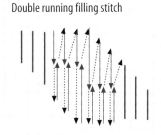

Double running filling stitch

Satin stitch features in most of the patterns sometimes with a smooth edge, at other times with a crenellated edge. If the stitch is too long it can be shortened by working part of the motif in double running filling stitch, see the Stephan pattern.

Satin Stitch

Double running stitch. The first line is worked over and under the required number of fabric threads. On the return journey it fills in the spaces left on the first.

Double running stitch

Both the **Long armed braid and Plaited Slav stitches** follow the numbered stitch movements. If wanting a deeper braid, take the needle under four threads instead of the three shown.

Plaited Slav stitch

1.   2.   3.

Long armed braid

1.   2.   3.   4.   5.

Antwerp edge stitch is a knotted buttonhole used to work a decorative edging around linen. To join two pieces together place them as required and work a second row of Antwerp edging into the loops of the first row.

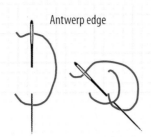

Antwerp edge

Antique hemstitch is used to hem linen. It is worked from left to right on the wrong side. Pick up the number of threads required from the hemstitch line, then anchor the thread into the folded turn under.

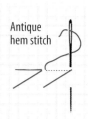

Antique hem stitch

Ladder stitch is used to join the mitred corners of hems together without the stitches showing. The needle slides down the inside of the fold and is carried straight across to the opposite side. Every few stitches tighten the thread to bring the two sides together.

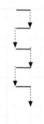

Trellis stitch

Trellis stitch is a detached filling stitch, used to cover the bobble.

1. Take the needle up into the fingercord where it enters the bobble.

2. Make a knot by bringing the needle back under the loop. Firm it up. There will be a link between each knot. On the following rows the needle is taken under the link as at 1. Increase and decrease the number of stitches as required.

1.

2.

To make a bobble

You will need: the thick top of pantyhose, cotton wool, tacking thread, tapestry and long darning needles. No. 8 perle cotton.

Instructions for a bobble

1. Cut a circle from the thick top of pantyhose; for a template use the round label in the No. 8 perle cotton ball, or 3 cm diameter. Run a gathering thread of small stitches around the edge.

2. This diagram shows that a piece of the cotton wool, the size required for a bobble has been placed on the pantyhose circle and the thread has been gathered and tied. For a secure hold, the ends have been stitched into the bobble. Use the head of a bodkin or similar to poke the gathered edge into the bobble.

3. To attach the finger cord to a bobble. Use a long darning needle to carry the threads from either a double or single length of finger cord through the centre of the bobble and out at the bottom. The short threads can be securely finished off in the bobble. Use the long darning needle and take a long thread back to the top and on a different route. Change to a tapestry needle. If two ends of finger cord, stab stitch to hold them together where they enter the bobble.

4. To cover the bobble work trellis stitch. The first round is linked into the fingercord and anchors it securely. Follow the diagrams above. Once the first row has been worked, increase the number of stitches for the following rows. When the trellis stitch is nearly long enough to cover the bobble, reduce the number of stitches made, until the bobble is covered and pulled into a ball. Finish the thread off in the bobble. Bring new threads up from the base as required.

5. To secure a thread cutter to a needlebook. Carry the two short threads into the bobble and secure them. Loop the other end of the finger cord under both the buttonhole loop at the spine of the needlebook and the thread cutter loop. Use a long darner to carry the two long threads into the bobble and use them to work trellis stitch as before.

Eyelets

are a feature of Ukrainian Whitework and are a factor in this style of needle work being different from most others. They come in a number of styles, shapes and sizes and are a pulled fabric technique. The eyelets both large and small are either worked in blocks or lines of varying lengths and widths, usually on the diagonal and sometimes as an outline to the pattern. Before beginning a project read the information given for each type of eyelet, then practise working them on a sampler.

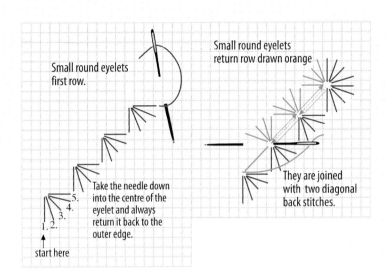

Small round eyelets first row.

Small round eyelets return row drawn orange

Take the needle down into the centre of the eyelet and always return it back to the outer edge.

5.
4.
3.
1. 2.

start here

They are joined with two diagonal back stitches.

To work eyelets note where to start on the colour coded pattern graph, use the tacking to count. Each graph line equals one thread. Take the needle and thread down into the centre of the eyelet and **always** return it back to the outer edge. If you get lost your needle and thread is most likely coming from the centre of the eyelet not the outer edge. Use No. 12 perle cotton or similar and have the linen firmly stretched in a small round frame.

To move to the next eyelet in the group take the needle down into the centre and bring it up into the centre of where the next one will be. Link them together with two diagonal back stitches as shown on the diagrams. Bring the needle back to the outer edge of the just completed eyelet and work the following one from there. The round eyelets are one thread less at the corners, this shapes them beautifully.

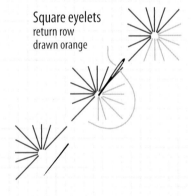

Square eyelets
return row
drawn orange

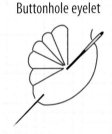

Buttonhole eyelet

The stitch sequence for buttonhole eyelets is shown on the Hala pattern graph

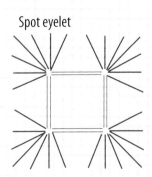

Spot eyelet

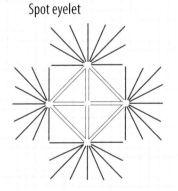

Spot eyelet

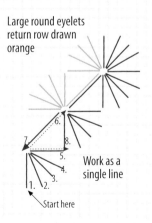

Large round eyelets return row drawn orange

6.
7.
8.
5.
4.
3.
1. 2.

Work as a single line

Start here

Large round eyelets

The diagrams are colour coded, and the stitch direction is marked with arrows. The black dotted lines show where the needle travels on the underside, the arrows where the needle enters the linen. The sequence the stitches are worked is numbered, not the steps. Some of the movements are back stitch, others similar to faggot stitch. The working thread is pulled and held down with the left thumb, at the same time opening the eyelet centre as large as possible.

Work the eyelets drawn red first, then the orange, next the green and finally the blue.

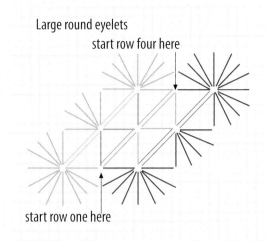

Large round eyelets

start row four here

start row one here

Start row one where shown and work around to the right. When the last straight stitch of the first eyelet is worked, carry the needle and thread under the cloth to where the second eyelet's centre will be and work two diagonal back stitches to link the first eyelet with the second. Return the needle back into the same space as the last straight stitch of the first eyelet at 2, turn 90° and work the first straight stitch of the second eyelet. Repeat until the last eyelet of row one, this time work three quarters way around as shown to be ready to begin row two.

The second row drawn orange is worked as a single faggot stitch. The third row drawn green is worked as both a faggot stitch and a diagonal back stitch. The fourth row drawn blue is a repeat of the first row drawn red.

The needle goes into the eyelet centre and is **always** returned back to the outer edge.

Turn the page for the diagrams to be in the direction required.

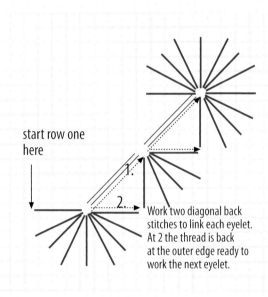

start row one here

1.
2.

Work two diagonal back stitches to link each eyelet. At 2 the thread is back at the outer edge ready to work the next eyelet.

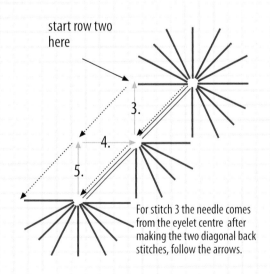

start row two here

3.
4.
5.

For stitch 3 the needle comes from the eyelet centre after making the two diagonal back stitches, follow the arrows.

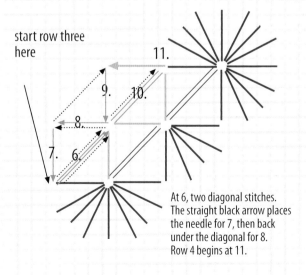

start row three here

11.
9. 10.
8.
7. 6.

At 6, two diagonal stitches. The straight black arrow places the needle for 7, then back under the diagonal for 8. Row 4 begins at 11.

Finger cords. This style of finger cord featured in a 1927 issue of *The Embroideress*.[1] They are an attractive, useful, functional method of finishing small projects and can be used as sturdy drawstrings to close lavender bags and similar items. Because finger cords are made with the same threads as the piece they will be applied to, they give a superior finishing touch. As a general guide when making finger cords cut the threads 4–6 times longer than the finished length required. This will give thread to attach the cord to a bobble, or similar and work much of the trellis stitch that covers it. Use any of the perle cottons and stranded cotton. For a finer cord use stranded cotton, each length three threads.

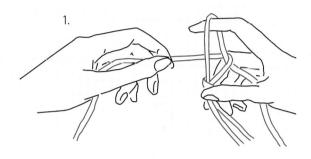

1.

❶ **To begin,** join the two lengths of thread together with a simple knot; leave 12 cm approximately to attach the cord to the bobble or similar.

Diagram 1. The thread is taken or twisted around the back of the loop to close it. The right hand thumb and second finger are holding the knot. The loop is held up by the first finger. The left hand is holding the second length of thread firm.

❷ Diagram 2. Put the first finger of your left hand into the loop on your right hand and lift the thread held in the left hand up. Take the first finger of your right hand out of the loop and pull the thread held in the right hand firmly to close the loop to make the knot. The loop is now held over the first finger of the left hand.

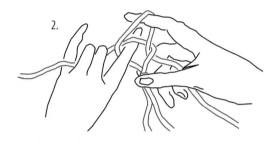

2.

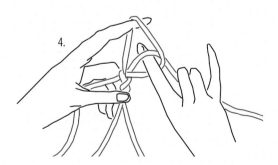

3.

❸ Diagram 3. Put the first finger of your right hand into the loop on your left hand then lift the thread held in the right hand up through the loop. Now pull the first finger on your left hand out of the loop and pull the thread held in the left hand to close the loop and make a knot.

❹ Repeat diagrams 2 and 3, changing hands from right to left, then left hand to right, until the length of cord required has been made. To secure the cord carry the thread through the loop and pull to close.

Remember when beginning, to take or twist the thread on the right hand around the back of the loop to close it.

Note the knot is always held by the thumb and second finger of the hand that has lifted the thread.

To practise making finger cords use two lengths of thick wool, each piece a different colour.

4.

Because of the method of working, extra thread is required for shorter cords.

[1] *The Embroideress*, 1922–1939, edited by Mrs J. D. Rolleston, published quarterly by James Pearsall & Co. Ltd. London. Annual subscription 10/8, post free UK and around the world.

Andrij Pattern

At the inner corners only turn on a three thread count

The outer blocks are 51 threads wide or 17 × 3 thread tacks

Spot eyelets

The small round eyelets are colour coded. Work the green portion first in a continuous line to establish the pattern, finish with the orange. Always return the needle and thread back to the outer edge.

Note the gap to give a 14 thread space for the spot eyelets

Tacking shown drawn black over 3 × 3 threads.
Each graph line equals one thread

Work small round eyelets to establish the pattern, begin on a tacked line 99 threads up from the centre tacking.

The inner blocks are 48 threads or 16 × 3 thread tacks out from the centre tacking line.

Centre tacking line through here, quarter not shown

Andrij PATTERN

Andrij (pronounced Andrey) like his forebears was a hard working successful farmer. He grew up at the beginning of the twentieth century and was active in many Ukrainian institutions, such as the Co-op society and Prosvita (enlightenment). The aim of Prosvita was to serve as a centre where village people could come together, meet socially, discuss matters of common interest and read newspapers. The centre included an amateur theatrical group, a choir, a library, self-educational centre and an opportunity for young people to meet at various functions. Under Polish occupation subjects such as Ukrainian history, literature, traditional folk dancing and even embroidery were not able to be taught, those subjects were provided by the self-educational groups. With the reoccupation of West Ukraine by the USSR, village life deteriorated disastrously. Many suffered harsh treatment for no cause during the brutal, turbulent times that followed.

The Andrij pattern is shown as a small square mat and has both drawn thread and narrow borders that would seem to be unique to Ukraine. The pattern is 48 threads wide × 30 threads deep and has two, three and four thread stitch units. The linen shown is 28 thread Cashel, colour 638 Olive Green. The threads are D.M.C. perle cottons Nos. 8 and 12, shade 524. The finished size is 24 cm square.

You will need:

- 28 count linen, 31 cm square
- Perle cottons No. 8 (2 balls) and No. 12
- Small round frame
- Tapestry and crewel needles
- Small sharp pointed scissors
- Colourfast tacking threads

The stitches and threads are:

- Work satin stitch, drawn thread and verkhoploot borders with No. 8 perle cotton.
- Small round eyelets, square spot eyelets, ladder hemstitch and antique hemstitch with No. 12 perle cotton.

Instructions:

- Read the useful information on linens, threads, tacking, etc., pages 17–21.
- Before proceeding read Drawn thread borders pages 104–109 for information and illustrations showing how to work these borders and deal with withdrawn threads. See option 4, page 106, for managing the inner border.
- Stitches, pages 22–25.
- Hems, page 111. Woven corner fillings, page 110.

Preparation:

- Straighten the linen and secure the raw edges.
- Tack a grid over 3 × 3 threads. It ensures accuracy and is a simple method for pattern placement.

To work the Andrij pattern use the colour coded graph. It includes the tacking shown as fine black lines. Begin on a centre tacking line and 99 threads or 33 × 3 thread tacks up from the centre and work the small round eyelets to establish the pattern. Follow the colour coding and work the side drawn

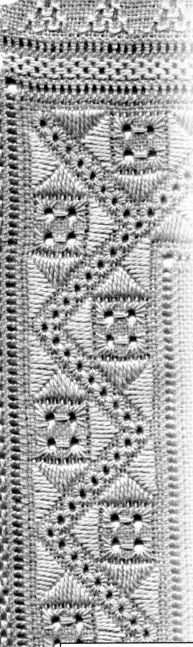

green first, then those drawn orange. Work the satin stitch blocks drawn red, they extend one thread beyond the small round eyelets.

- There is a gap at the corners to give a 14 thread space to work the square spot eyelets.
- Where the sides meet at the inner corners turn on a three thread count.

Drawn thread borders working instructions, stitches and borders are on pages 104–109.

- Allow 62 threads for the drawn thread, narrow borders and hem.

From the centre of a side the stitch sequence and borders to be worked are:

- Leave one thread between the main pattern and drawn thread border.
- Leave 2 threads, cut 2, leave 2 and work ladder hemstitch across these six threads.
- Cut four threads for needle weaving, they are not withdrawn until both rows of ladder hemstitch have been worked.
- Leave 2 threads, cut 2, leave 2 and work ladder hemstitch across them.
- It is important to have the hemstitches gathering the same threads into bundles of two.

Once the withdrawn threads are hanging loose at the corner, darn every second one back to the edge of the cloth, see pages 104–107.

The Needle woven border is No. 7 and known in Ukraine as Merezhka Verkhoploot. It is worked with No. 8 perle cotton over the four cut and withdrawn threads from left to right and always in the same direction. The method of working is the same as smocking. See page 108.

Corners: the photograph shows they have been left open, if required a small filling could be worked, see page 110.

Verkhoploot narrow border edges the drawn thread borders, see page 103.

Hem is 22 threads deep and includes the verkhoploot narrow border, tack the lines required, see page 111. Mitre the corners. Hemstitch is worked over 2 × 2 threads and into the ladder hemstitch that borders the drawn threads.

Embroider your name and date on the reverse side of the hem in a simple back stitch.

Well done! You have completed a beautiful piece of Ukrainian Whitework that would make a lovely gift for someone special.

Andrij tacking grid & pattern layout

Quarter 31 cm square cloth shown.
Tack 3 × 3 threads, shown as dotted lines.
Pattern blocks 48 threads wide × 32 threads deep, shown as solid lines.

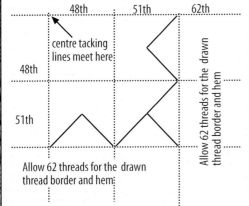

48th · 51th · 62th

centre tacking lines meet here

48th

51th

Allow 62 threads for the drawn thread border and hem

Allow 62 threads for the drawn thread border and hem

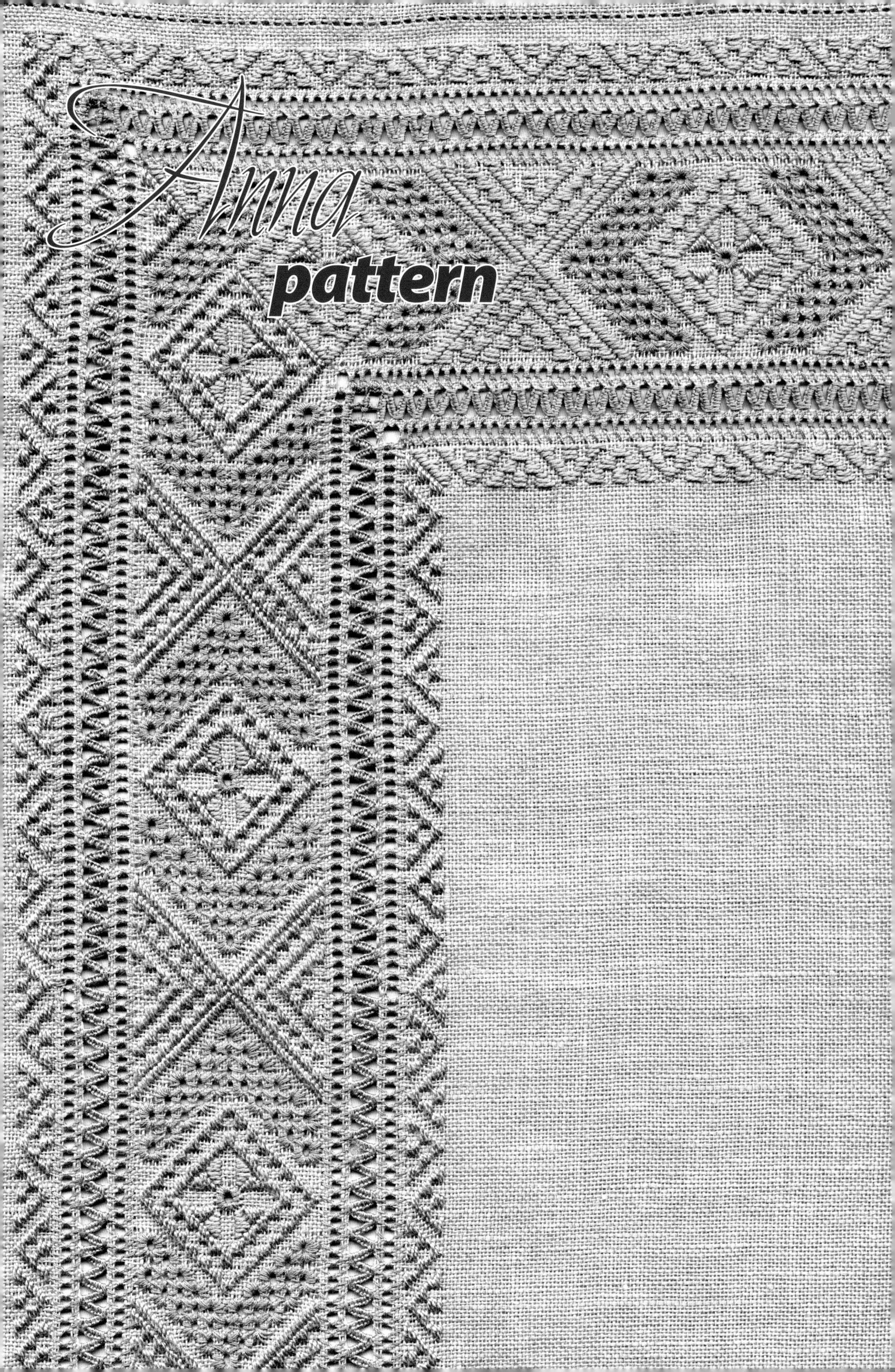
Anna
pattern

Anna Pattern

Each graph line equals one thread.

Read the pattern this way up.
Drawn thread borders will be worked
on both sides of the pattern.

The tacking is over 4 × 4
threads drawn black.
Pattern width 52 threads,
depth 48 threads.

Allow about 68 threads
beyond the tacking for the
drawn thread, narrow
borders and hem. See the
photograph, it shows two
rows of ladder hemstitch
with zig-zag buttonhole
stitch worked between
and a narrow border.

The centre of each side of
a square mat, see photo-
graph. Work this large mot
with No. 8 perle cotton, eit
begin at the centre where
the tacking threads meet,
or count the tacks at the
outer edge drawn black to
begin the satin stitch, drav
green.

Start large round eyelets
here, work with No. 12
perle cotton or similar.
Begin with those drawn
red, then orange, next
green, finish with blue.

A large round eyelet
worked with No. 12
perle cotton is
worked at the centre
of this motif.

This small portion
drawn green shows
how the two diamond
motifs link when
turning a corner.
See the photograph.

Anna PATTERN

The night Anna's husband Andrij did not come home was the beginning of a nightmare for her and her family. In 1944 Andrij was caught by the Russian military in a street roundup some miles from their home and taken to the Lithuanian front near the Baltic sea. He was hit by shrapnel on the lower jaw and eventually taken to a Russian military hospital. Due to shock and blood loss he suffered amnesia. Having no identification he simply became a number. Because Andrij was taken off the street, nobody knew what had happened to him. Local KGB agents accused Anna that her husband had joined the Ukrainian Insurgent army (UPA) which was active in Western Ukraine up till 1950. Eventually Andrij regained his memory and was discharged. He came back with part of his jaw bone missing, took his wife and daughter home and restored some semblance of normality to their lives. Because of the activities of the UPA, life was not at all easy for Anna's family. They were constantly brought in for questioning and threatened with a gun at their temples. In spite of all this Anna and Andrij lived to celebrate their 64th wedding anniversary.

The Anna pattern is shown as a square table centre with a 9 cm deep border worked around the four sides. It has a drawn thread border worked on each side of the main pattern and a small narrow border beyond that. The finished size is 42 cm square. The linen shown is Semco 30 count, colour steel blue. The threads used are Anchor perle cotton No. 8, shade 1034, Anchor stranded cotton shade 1034 and Coats Duet sewing cotton, shade 89.

You will need:

- 30 count linen 45 cm × 45 cm
- Perle cotton No. 8 (2 balls), stranded cotton (3 skeins), Coats Duet sewing cotton (2 reels) or No. 12 perle cotton
- Small round frame, tapestry and crewel needles
- Small sharp pointed scissors, tacking threads

The stitches and threads used are:

- Satin stitch is worked with No. 8 perle cotton.
- Large round eyelets and ladder hemstitch with Coats Duet sewing cotton.
- Drawn thread zig zag buttonhole and corner filling with two strands of stranded cotton.
- The hem is worked with threads withdrawn from the linen.

Instructions:

- Stitches, see pages 22–25.
- Read the useful information on linen threads, tacking, etc., pages 17–21.
- Important to read Drawn thread borders, pages 104–107, for information, photographs and instructions showing how to work these borders and deal with withdrawn threads. The inner borders are worked before the pattern can be stitched at the corners.
- Hems, page 111. Woven filling, page 110.

Preparation:

- Straighten the linen and secure the raw edges.
- Tack a grid over 4 × 4 threads. It ensures accuracy and is a simple method for pattern placement.

- The pattern is 48 threads deep × 52 threads wide. The drawn thread and narrow borders enlarge it to 112 threads deep.
- To work the Anna pattern use the colour coded graph, it includes the tacking shown as fine black lines. The pattern is started at the centre of a side with the large motif. Use the tacking shown on the graph to place it across the centre. The pattern layout shows how the two diamond motifs link at the corner.

Work the large round eyelets with Coats Duet sewing cotton. Use it double.

Drawn thread, narrow border and hem are worked over the 68–72 threads beyond the tacked pattern edge; the count includes the machine neatened cut edge.

The drawn thread border is worked up to the tacked pattern edge. From the centre of a side the stitch sequence and borders to be worked are:

- Leave 3 threads, cut 2, leave 3 and work the ladder hemstitch across these eight threads.
- Cut 6 threads, they are not withdrawn until edged with ladder hemstitch. The drawn thread border is No. 6 zig zag buttonhole stitch, page 108.
- Leave 3 threads, cut 2, leave 3 and work a second row of ladder hemstitch.
- Important to have each row of hemstitch gathering the same threads across the border into bundles of three.
- Once the withdrawn threads are hanging loose at the corner, darn every second one out to the edge of the cloth, see pages 104–107.

To complete the corner, work large round eyelets across the corner to the count shown on the graph, then a small portion of the satin stitch, see the photograph.

Narrow border. The one shown is No. 7, page 102.

Corner filling. Use the sewing thread left from the zig zag buttonhole stitch to work a simple filling.

Hem. Count the threads from the edge of border out to the hem edge and tack to mark the hem lines required. Allow a 12 thread hem with a 6–8 thread turn under. Mitre the corners and hemstitch over three threads.

Work your name and date on the reverse side of the hem in a simple back stitch.

Well done! You have completed a beautiful piece of Ukrainian Whitework that will become a family heirloom.

Anna tacking grid and pattern layout

Tack 4 × 4 threads, pattern blocks 48 threads deep and 52 threads wide. Quarter 45 cm square cloth shown. Drawn thread and narrow border worked both sides of the pattern.

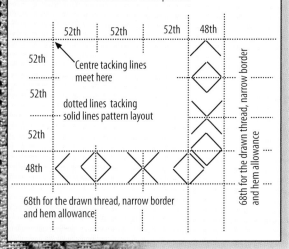

Centre tacking lines meet here

dotted lines tacking
solid lines pattern layout

52th | 52th | 52th | 48th

52th
52th
52th
48th

68th for the drawn thread, narrow border and hem allowance

Daria **pattern**

Daria Pattern

Narrow border 36 threads wide, the pattern continues on the right hand side of this page

Each graph line equals one thread

Continue here, overlap & link with the left hand side

Begin the pattern here at the centre

Centre tacking

The 3×3 thread tacking drawn as fine black lines each side of the border. The eyelets are accurate to the tacking.

To continue, begin again at the top left hand side and repeat the pattern.

This space separates the two portions of the 36 thread wide border

Daria PATTERN

Embroidery permeates the life of every Ukrainian whether it is in the social sphere, religious life, customs or just simply for love of it. One of the customs was when a young man was leaving home his girlfriend gave him as a memento an embroidered kerchief, his mother either an embroidered rushnyk (ritual cloth) or a shirt. There is a song set to lyrics that bring up the analogy of the life of every involuntary migrant who had to leave home for fear of his or her life. The lyrics say that when he was leaving home his mother gave him a shirt she had embroidered with red and black threads. When he returned home through once familiar paths he still held in his hands remnants of the shirt upon which his life was embroidered with threads of red and black. Red was for love and black had many meanings including sorrow, sadness, grief, remorse, anticipation of unknown and similar all rolled into one.

The Daria pattern is shown as a small runner with the pattern worked through the centre of the cloth. It includes a drawn thread border and a narrow border of verkhoploot to edge the piece. The finished size is 41 cm × 8 cm or 16″ × 7″.

The linen shown is a 30 count Semco shade Mallow, the threads Anchor perle cottons No. 8, No. 12 and stranded cotton, each shade 926.

You will need:
- Runner: 45 cm × 22 cm
- Perle cottons No. 8, No.12 and stranded cotton
- Small round frame
- Tapestry and crewel needles
- Small sharp pointed scissors
- Tacking threads

The stitches and threads are:
- Satin stitch is worked with No. 8 perle.
- Reverse faggot, square eyelets, verkhoploot border and ladder hemstitch with No. 12 perle.
- Drawn thread zig zag buttonhole use two strands of stranded cotton.

Instructions:
- Read the useful information for linen threads, tacking, etc., pages 17–21.
- Stitches, see pages 22–25.
- Important to read Drawn thread borders, pages 104–107, for information and photographs showing how to work these borders and deal with withdrawn threads.
- Hems, page 111.
- Woven corner filling, page 110.

Preparation:
- Straighten the linen and secure the raw edges.
- Tack an accurate grid 3 × 3 threads to find the centre of the cloth. It ensures accuracy and is a simple method for pattern placement.
- Tack the two outer lines, they are 18 threads out from the centre.

To work the Daria pattern use the colour coded graph, it includes the tacking shown as fine black lines. The Daria pattern is 36 threads wide and 240 threads long and has both three and four thread stitch units.

Work the square eyelets; they are colour coded to show that each side is worked in a continuous line. Use this as a guide and not the only route to take.

The satin stitch is worked over four threads, note the change of count at the corners. Work the two rows of double reverse faggot with the square eyelets between.

Drawn thread border is worked up to the tacked outer edge of the pattern. It is border No. 6, zig zag buttonhole, page 108. The working instructions, stitches and patterns are on pages 104–107. See options 2 and 3, page 106, for managing the short end border.

From the centre of a side the stitch sequence and borders to be worked are:

- Leave 3 threads, cut 2, leave 3 and work ladder hemstitch across these 8 threads.
- Cut six, they are not withdrawn until both rows of ladder hemstitch are worked. Zig zag buttonhole stitch will be worked across them.
- Leave 3, cut 2 , leave 3 for a second row of ladder hemstitch.
- It is important to have the hemstitches gathering the same threads across the border into bundles.

Once the withdrawn threads are hanging loose at the corners, darn every second one back to the edge of the cloth, see pages 104–107 for instructions.

Corner filling: use the stranded cotton left from the zig zag buttonhole border to lay diagonally back and forth across the corner three times. Work buttonhole stitch over this bar and anchor it to follow on from the rest of the drawn thread border, see the photograph.

A verkhoploot border is worked around the edge of the drawn thread border and one thread out from the ladder hemstitch. Work the long sides first. Once they are completed, work the short sides. Begin at the right hand side and work the base row of straight stitches to the end of the left side. Work back over the base stitches to complete each triangle as the diagrams show. This useful border would seem to be unique to Ukraine. See the diagrams page 103.

Hem, count the threads from edge of the border out to hem edge, tack to mark the lines required. Mitre the corners and work hemstitch over 3 × 3 threads with threads withdrawn from the linen.

Work your name and date on the reverse side of the hem in a simple back stitch.

Well done! You have completed a lovely piece of Ukrainian Whitework that will be admired and enjoyed.

Daria tacking grid & pattern layout

Tack 3 × 3 threads

Cloth Centre

36thds

Pattern worked along the 36 threads at the centre

Eugenie
pattern

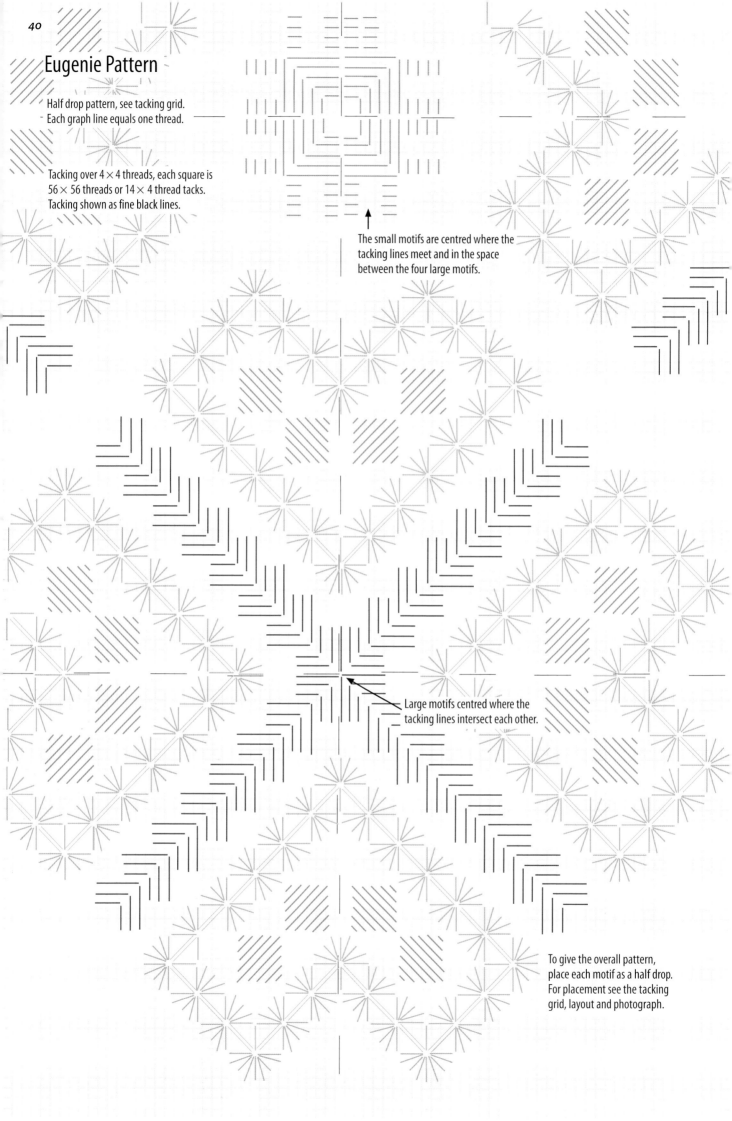

Eugenie Pattern

Half drop pattern, see tacking grid.
Each graph line equals one thread.

Tacking over 4 × 4 threads, each square is
56 × 56 threads or 14 × 4 thread tacks.
Tacking shown as fine black lines.

The small motifs are centred where the
tacking lines meet and in the space
between the four large motifs.

Large motifs centred where the
tacking lines intersect each other.

To give the overall pattern,
place each motif as a half drop.
For placement see the tacking
grid, layout and photograph.

Eugenie PATTERN

Eugenie's story is one which happened to many Ukrainian children during WWII and the German occupation of their country. One day the German authorities turned up in Eugenie's village and took teenagers to work in their munitions factories in Germany. They had to leave straight away without being able to say good-bye to family and friends. Eugenie's older sister, Marenka, was supposed to go but as she had a sore foot Eugenie went instead. They were checked out by a doctor and the next day started working in a factory and remained there until the end of the Second World War, May 1945. The young people were then taken to a camp that was under British occupation, told that they could go back to Ukraine, but many did not want to because Ukraine was again under communist rule. Instead Eugenie and the sweetheart she had met in the camp chose to take the opportunity to go to Australia and make a new life for themselves on the other side of the world.

The Eugenie pattern is worked in the centre of a square mat; it features both large and small motifs placed over a tacked grid to give a half drop pattern. The finished size is 40 cm square.

The linen shown is 28 count Semco, shade off white. The threads Anchor perle cottons No. 8 shade 386, No. 12 shade 2.

You will need:

- 28 count linen, 45 cm × 45 cm
- Perle cottons No. 8 and No. 12
- Small round frame
- Tapestry and crewel needles
- Small sharp pointed scissors
- Tacking threads

The stitches and threads are:

- Satin stitch is worked with No 8 perle cotton.
- Small round eyelets, ladder hemstitch, picot edge and hemstitching with No. 12 perle cotton.

Instructions:

- Read the useful information on linen threads, tacking, etc., pages 17–21.
- Stitches, see pages 22–25.
- Ladder hemstitch, page 105.
- Hems, page 111.
- Important to read Drawn thread borders, pages 104–107, for information and photographs showing how to work them and deal with withdrawn threads.

Preparation:

- Straighten the linen and secure the raw edges.
- Tack an accurate grid over 4 × 4 threads. It ensures accuracy and is a simple method for pattern placement.
- Begin at the centre and tack a grid of squares, each block where the tacking meets is 56 threads square or 14 × 4 thread tacks. The tacking grid and pattern layout clearly show the half drop pattern placement of both the large and small motifs.

To work the Eugenie pattern follow the colour coded graph, it includes the tacking drawn as fine black lines. Work both the large and small motifs. They are satin stitch with a crenellated edge, each is centred where the tacking lines intersect each other.

The heart shapes are small round eyelets. First work the outer row drawn blue, then inner row drawn orange. Four small satin stitch squares fill the heart shapes.

Hem. Use the centre tacking lines to count the threads from edge of the pattern out to edge of the linen. Make any adjustments to make sure that the hem will be the same number of threads on each side of the cloth from the pattern.

- Tack both the hem edge and the turn under lines, see page 111.

Picot edge:

- Work ladder hemstitch up to the hem edge tacking and across the eight threads towards the cloth centre, see page 105.

- Cut and withdraw the two threads required for ladder hemstitch back to the corner to meet with the two threads from the adjoining side. Darn every second one out to the edge of the cloth, see pages 104–107 for instructions.

- Work ladder hemstitch each side of the cloth.

- Fold the ladder hemstitch in half to give a lovely picot hem edge that requires no further stitching.

- Fold the hem turn under line on the tacking.

- Mitre the corners and work hemstitch over 3 × 3 threads and 12 threads in from the picot edge.

Work your name and date on the reverse side of the hem in a simple back stitch.

Well done! You have completed a lovely piece of Ukrainian Whitework that will be admired and enjoyed for many years.

The Eugenie tacking grid and half drop pattern layout

Half 45 cm square cloth shown. Tack 4 × 4 threads, each tacked square is 56 × 56 threads or 14 × 4 thread tacks. The motifs both large and small are centred where the tacking lines meet.

Centre, tacking lines meet here

Tacking shown as dotted lines, solid lines pattern placement. Allow 86 threads beyond this tacking to include the picot edged hem.

Hala Pattern

Each graph line equals one thread

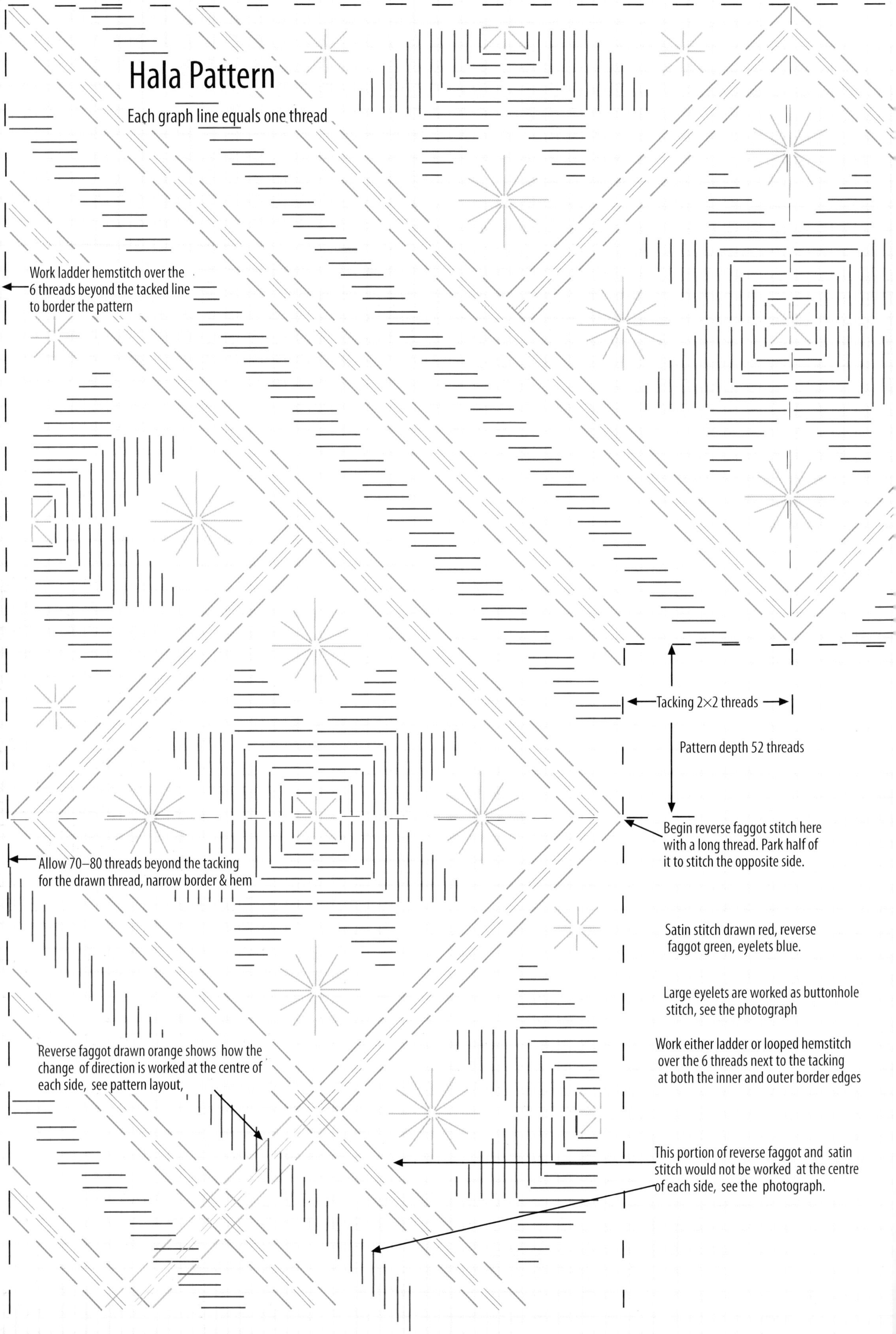

Work ladder hemstitch over the 6 threads beyond the tacked line to border the pattern

Tacking 2×2 threads

Pattern depth 52 threads

Begin reverse faggot stitch here with a long thread. Park half of it to stitch the opposite side.

Allow 70–80 threads beyond the tacking for the drawn thread, narrow border & hem

Satin stitch drawn red, reverse faggot green, eyelets blue.

Large eyelets are worked as buttonhole stitch, see the photograph

Work either ladder or looped hemstitch over the 6 threads next to the tacking at both the inner and outer border edges

Reverse faggot drawn orange shows how the change of direction is worked at the centre of each side, see pattern layout,

This portion of reverse faggot and satin stitch would not be worked at the centre of each side, see the photograph.

$\mathcal{H}ala$ PATTERN

After World War I and losing their fight for independence Ukraine was divided. The eastern part became one of the 15 Republics of the USSR and the Western part, where Hala's family had lived for many generations, became part of Poland. They had a good life until 1939 when the Soviet Russian army liberated them from Polish oppression. The liberators stripped the people of their possessions and terror stalked the land. In 1941 Germany declared war on the USSR and life was a little better in West Ukraine, except for the Jewish people who suffered badly under German occupation. By 1948 Hala was in a 'Displaced Persons' camp in West Germany when the Australian Government offered Ukrainian refugees asylum on the other side of the world. After two years living in a 'worker's paradise' Hala gladly and gratefully took this opportunity to get away as far as she could from Communist Russia, and promised herself that she would never be hungry and cold again.

The Hala pattern is a small square mat worked on 28 count Permin linen, shade rose pink. The D.M.C perle cottons Nos. 8 and 12 are shade 223. The finished size is 33 cm square.

You will need:

- 28 count linen, 40 cm × 40 cm, perle cottons No. 8 (2 balls) and No. 12
- Small round frame, tapestry and crewel needles
- Small sharp pointed scissors, tacking threads

The stitches and threads are:

Satin stitch, buttonhole eyelets, small square eyelets and verkhoploot border are worked with No. 8 perle cotton. Reverse faggot, ladder hemstitch, needle wrapped border and woven corner filling with No. 12 perle cotton.

Instructions:

- Read the useful information on linen threads, tacking, etc., pages 17–21.
- Before proceeding read Drawn thread borders, pages 104–107, for information and photographs showing how to work these borders and deal with withdrawn threads.
- Stitches, see pages 22–25. Hems, page 111. Corner fillings, pages 110.

Preparation:

- Straighten the linen and secure the raw edges.
- Tack an accurate grid over 2 × 2 threads.
- Tack to find the centre and use it to find the stitching line, 94 threads up from the centre of the cloth.
- The Hala pattern is 52 threads deep. A further 70–80 threads beyond the main pattern is required for the drawn thread, narrow border and hem.
- The tacking grid, pattern layout and photograph clearly show the method of changing direction at the centre of each side to allow the lines of reverse faggot stitching and satin stitch to work towards each corner.
- The lines of stitching between the reverse faggot can be changed to suit, they could each be different forms of satin stitch, or choose to work various line stitches. If working on a more open weave an extra line of stitching could be added to give a closer effect.

To work the Hala pattern use the colour coded graph. It includes the tacking drawn as fine black lines and also shows the change of count for the various

portions. Work the two long diagonal lines of double reverse faggot stitch; begin each line at the pattern centre and work towards the corners, see the pattern layout and note that the reverse faggot stitch changes direction on a V point. Cut a longer length of thread and leave half of it parked in the linen. Stitch the first long diagonal line to meet the tacking on the opposite side. Turn and work back to nearly at the beginning, this time the stitching will be on the inside of the line. Re-thread the needle with the parked thread and work the second line of reverse faggot stitch out in the other direction. See reverse faggot stitch, page 22, with instructions for the change of direction.

To complete the central diamond, begin as before on the centre tacking; have a longer length of thread and use half to work out in one direction to join with the longer line. Re-thread the needle and work the other half to complete that portion. The extra length of thread used half at a time avoids having to finish off two threads.

Follow the graph to place the satin stitch florets and buttonhole eyelets.

Drawn thread border is worked one thread out from the tacked pattern edge. The working instructions, stitches and patterns are on pages 104–109.

From the centre of a side the cutting sequence and borders to be worked are:

- Leave 2 threads, cut 2, leave 2 and work ladder hemstitch across these 6 threads
- Cut 6 threads. They are not withdrawn until edged with ladder hemstitch. The needle wrapped border worked across them is No. 11, page 109.
- Leave 2 threads, cut 2, leave 2 and work a second row of ladder hemstitch.
- It is important to have the hemstitches gathering the same threads across the border into bundles of two.
- The photograph shows that ladder hemstitch is also worked at the edge of the inner border. See option 4, page 106, for dealing with those threads.

Once the withdrawn threads are hanging loose at the corners, darn every second one back to the edge of the cloth.

Woven corner filling. Use the No. 12 perle cotton left from the drawn thread border, see page 110.

A verkhoploot border is worked around the edge of the drawn thread border and two threads beyond the ladder stitch, see the photograph. The diagrams are on page 103.

Hem. Count the threads from edge of the border out to the hem edge, tack to mark the three lines required. The photograph shows a 22 thread deep hem that includes the verkhoploot border. Mitre the corners and hemstitch over 2 × 2 threads with threads withdrawn from the linen. It is worked into the outer edge of the ladder hemstitch border.

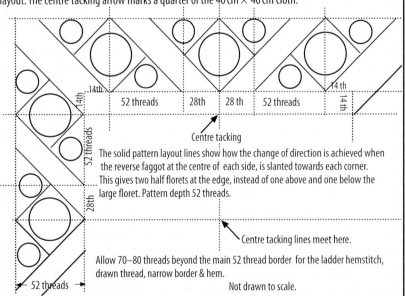

Hala tacking diagram and pattern layout

The 2 × 2 thread tacking is shown as dotted lines. The solid lines and thread count show the pattern layout. The centre tacking arrow marks a quarter of the 40 cm × 40 cm cloth.

14th | 52 threads | 28th | 28th | 52 threads | 14 th

14th · 52 threads · 28th

Centre tacking

The solid pattern layout lines show how the change of direction is achieved when the reverse faggot at the centre of each side, is slanted towards each corner. This gives two half florets at the edge, instead of one above and one below the large floret. Pattern depth 52 threads.

Centre tacking lines meet here.

Allow 70–80 threads beyond the main 52 thread border for the ladder hemstitch, drawn thread, narrow border & hem.

← 52 threads →

Not drawn to scale.

Well done! You have completed a lovely piece of Ukrainian Whitework that will be admired and enjoyed for many years.

Iryna **pattern**

Iryna Pattern

Each graph line equals one thread.
The 4 × 4 thread tacking is drawn black.
The pattern blocks are 44 × 44 threads

It is helpful to tack the direction that each satin stitch
diagonal motif lays. Begin at a corner. See the tacking
grid and pattern layout.

Start the large round eyelets here, work the first shown
red, then the orange, follow with the green and finish
with blue. Use the tacking as a guide.

Drawn thread borders are worked at the tacked edge,
both sides of the pattern and across 28 threads. See
photograph. Ladder hemstitch is worked across
8 × 3 threads and at both sides of a 12 thread
needlewoven border.

A narrow border and hem are worked on the 48–50
threads beyond the drawn thread borders.

Iryna PATTERN

Before Iryna started school, her grandmother had taught her to sew on buttons and make simple stitches. At school her embroidery teacher was the wife of their village priest and she taught the young children simple stitches to work on household linen and doll's clothes. The women and the older girls of the village embroidered their beautiful garments worn for festival occasions while the most experienced worked the linen and vestments for their local church. During the winter months they would gather together and sit around the fire to stitch, sing songs and tell stories of their heroes and heroines from past generations. Ukraine did its utmost under exceptionally difficult circumstances to keep its culture alive and celebrated whenever they could by enjoying good food and wearing their embroidered clothing for special occasions and to concerts.

The Iryna pattern is shown as a square mat with a 9 cm deep border worked around the four sides. The main border is edged with needle weaving and the outer edge has a narrow satin stitch border. The finished size is 41 cm square.

The linen shown is 28 count, Semco Old White, the threads, Anchor perle cottons No. 8 and No. 12, shade 387.

You will need:

- 28 count linen, 45 cm × 45 cm
- Perle cottons No. 8 (2 balls) and No. 12
- Small round frame
- Tapestry and crewel needles
- Small sharp pointed scissors
- Tacking threads

The stitches and threads used are:

- Satin stitch, needleweaving and narrow border are worked with No. 8 perle cotton.
- Large round eyelets, ladder hemstitch and hemstitch with No. 12 perle.

Instructions:

- Read the useful information on linen threads, tacking, etc., pages 17–21.
- Important to read Drawn thread borders, pages 104–109, for information, photographs and instructions showing how to work these borders and deal with withdrawn threads. See options 2 and 3, page 106, for managing the inner border.
- For stitches see pages 22–25.
- Hems, page 111. Woven corner fillings, page 110.

Preparation:

- Straighten the linen and secure the raw edges.
- Tack an accurate grid over 4 × 4 threads. It ensures accuracy and is a simple method for pattern placement.
- The pattern is 44 threads deep and 44 threads wide.
- The Iryna pattern requires an even number of blocks. It is helpful to tack the direction that each diagonal satin stitch motif lays, begin at a corner and work around the mat.
- The inner drawn thread borders are completed before the pattern can be stitched at the corners.

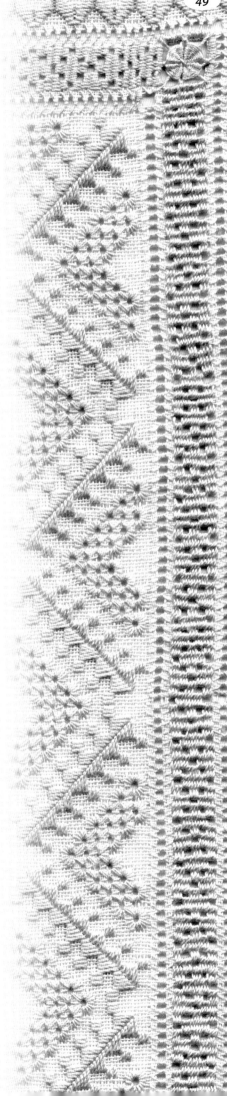

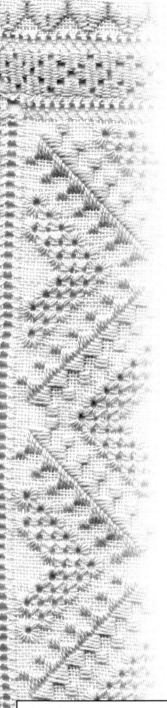

To work the Iryna pattern use the colour coded graph. It includes the tacking drawn as fine black lines. Begin at the centre of a side and work the satin stitch diagonal lines. Work the large round eyelets as shown drawn on the graph, the working instructions are on page 25. Leave the corners unstitched until the inner drawn thread borders have been completed.

Drawn thread is worked on both sides of this border; it is 28 threads deep and is worked up to the tacking lines. Before cutting any inner threads, measure to check that there will be at least twice the length of fabric thread to darn out to the cut edge of the cloth, from the centre tacking. Use the tacking as a guide. If not long enough, see drawn thread option 2 and option 3, page 106 — they give two useful methods to deal with this.

From the centre of a side the stitch sequence and borders worked are :

- Leave 3 threads, cut 2, leave 3 and work ladder hemstitch across these 8 threads.
- Cut 12, they are not withdrawn until edged with ladder hemstitch. The needle woven border is No. 3, page 107.
- Leave 3, cut 2, leave 3 and work a second row of ladder hemstitch.
- It is important to have the hemstitches gathering the same three threads across the border into bundles.

Once the withdrawn threads are hanging loose at the corner, darn every second one back to the edge of the linen, see page 104–107.

Woven corner filling. Use the No. 12 perle left from the ladder hemstitch. Lay horizontal and vertical threads across the open space. Weave across three threads as shown page 110.

Narrow border, the one illustrated is No. 10 on page 102. It is worked around the outer edge only.

Hems. Count the threads from edge of the border out to the hem edge, tack to mark the hem lines required. Mitre the corners and work hemstitch over 3 × 3 threads with perle cotton or threads withdrawn from the linen.

Work your name and date on the reverse side of the hem in a simple back stitch.

Well done! You have completed a lovely piece of Ukrainian Whitework that will become a treasured family heirloom.

Iryna tacking grid and pattern layout

Quarter 45 cm sq cloth shown.
Tack 4 × 4 threads shown as dotted lines. Pattern layout shown as solid lines in the 44 × 44 thread blocks.

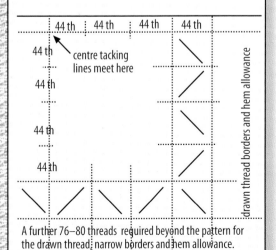

| 44 th | 44 th | 44 th | 44 th |

44 th — centre tacking lines meet here

44 th

44 th

44 th

drawn thread borders and hem allowance

A further 76–80 threads required beyond the pattern for the drawn thread, narrow borders and hem allowance.

Kateryna Pattern

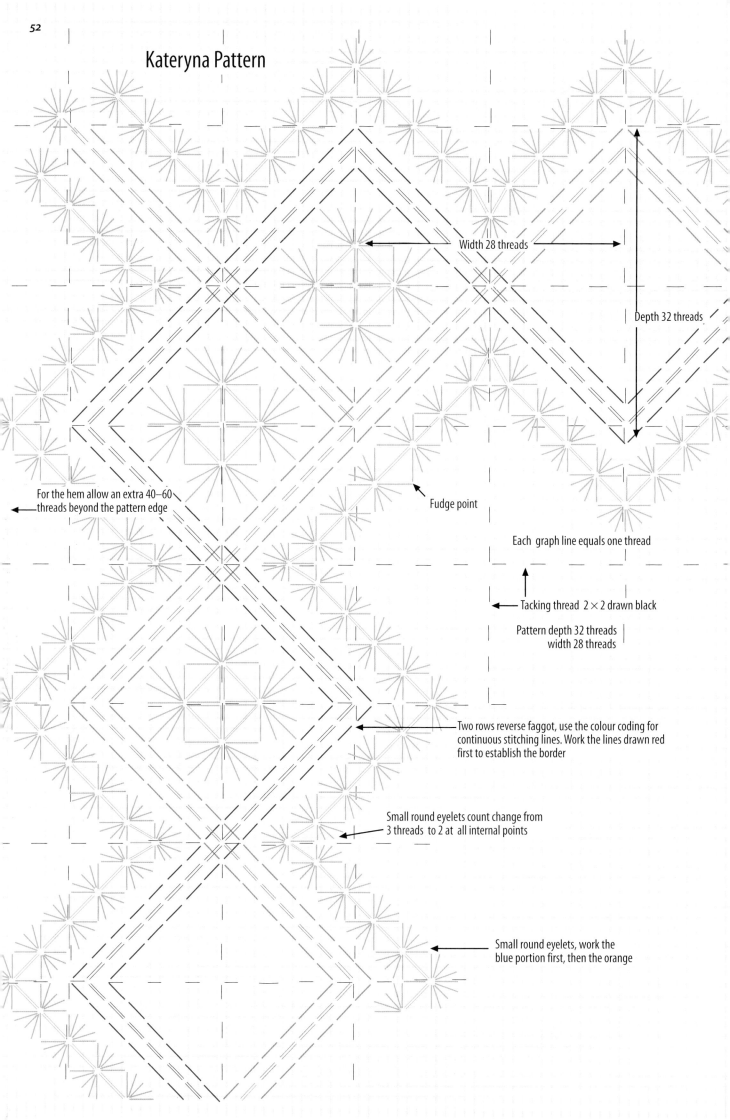

Width 28 threads

Depth 32 threads

For the hem allow an extra 40–60 threads beyond the pattern edge

Fudge point

Each graph line equals one thread

Tacking thread 2 × 2 drawn black

Pattern depth 32 threads
width 28 threads

Two rows reverse faggot, use the colour coding for continuous stitching lines. Work the lines drawn red first to establish the border

Small round eyelets count change from 3 threads to 2 at all internal points

Small round eyelets, work the blue portion first, then the orange

Kateryna PATTERN

For many generations Kateryna's family had farmed 100 km from Kyiv. They grew wheat and vegetables, worked hard and made a good living. In 1929 all that changed when the USSR communist regime brought in a policy of collectivisation that changed the lifestyle for many thousands of Ukrainian farmers and their families. All private farms, buildings, animals and grains were confiscated; instead the people had to work on collective farms as directed and were only paid meagre wages. Those who refused were deported to Siberia as 'Enemies of the People of Soviet Union' and called 'Kulaks', because they were considered to have been wealthy farmers. Kateryna's father and grandfather suffered that fate.

The Kateryna pattern is shown as a small runner. It has two, three and four thread stitch units and a fudge point at the inner corner, marked on the graphed pattern. This count change is a feature of Ukrainian Whitework that gives it a special charm and beauty. The finished size is 23 cm × 12 cm.

The linen shown is a 25 count Lauder, shade Old White purchased many years ago. The threads used are D.M.C. perle cottons Nos. 8 and 12, shade 644.

You will need:

- 25 count linen, 65 cm × 35 cm
- Perle cottons No. 8 and No. 12 (2 balls)
- Small round frame
- Tapestry and crewel needles
- Small sharp pointed scissors
- Tacking threads

The stitches and threads used are:

- Large square eyelet blocks are stitched with No. 8 perle cotton.
- Reverse faggot and small round eyelets with No. 12 perle cotton.
- The hem is stitched with threads withdrawn from the linen.

Instructions:

- Read the useful information on linen threads, tacking, etc., pages 17–21.
- For stitches see pages 22–25.
- Hems, page 111. Woven corner fillings, page 110.

Preparation:

- Straighten the linen and secure the raw edges.
- Tack an accurate grid over 2 × 2 threads. It ensures accuracy and is a simple method for pattern placement.
- The pattern is 32 threads deep × 28 threads wide. Two threads on either side of the width are linked to their neighbour; this gives the outer patterns a different count.
- Tack the number of blocks required 28 threads out from the centre or last tacked line.
- Note that the outer block is 32 threads out from the previous tacking, see the graphed pattern.

To work the Kateryna pattern follow the colour coded graph. It includes the tacking drawn as fine black lines and clearly shows the pattern placement.

To establish the pattern work reverse faggot stitch. The rows are colour coded to illustrate how it travels. The accurate tacking shows where to change direction and length of stitching into the corners.

Small round eyelets. Note there are two changes to thread count when working them; this is because the pattern is not worked over a universal thread count. The changes are clearly marked and drawn on the graphed pattern.

- At all inner corners the count changes from the usual three to two threads.
- There is a 'fudge point' where the length and width meet. One eyelet only is worked over four threads. This will not show unless pointed out.

Large square eyelet blocks fill each centre. Each eyelet within the block is linked by two diagonal back stitches, see page 24.

Hem. Count the threads from edge of the border out to the hem edge, tack to mark the three lines required. Mitre the corners and work hemstitch over 2 × 2 threads.

Work your name and date on the reverse side of the hem in a simple back stitch.

Well done! You have completed a lovely piece of Ukrainian Whitework that will be admired and enjoyed for many years.

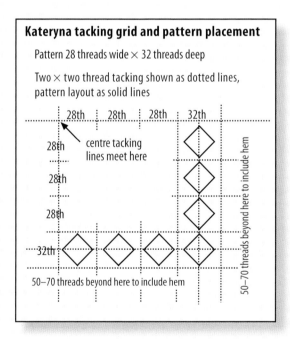

Kateryna tacking grid and pattern placement

Pattern 28 threads wide × 32 threads deep

Two × two thread tacking shown as dotted lines, pattern layout as solid lines

Maria **pattern**

Maria Pattern

96 threads square

Each graph line equals one thread.

Tacking 3 × 3 threads
pattern centre line ➡

Start eyelets 18 threads down from the tacked outer edge.

Tacked outer edge
Pattern edge ➡

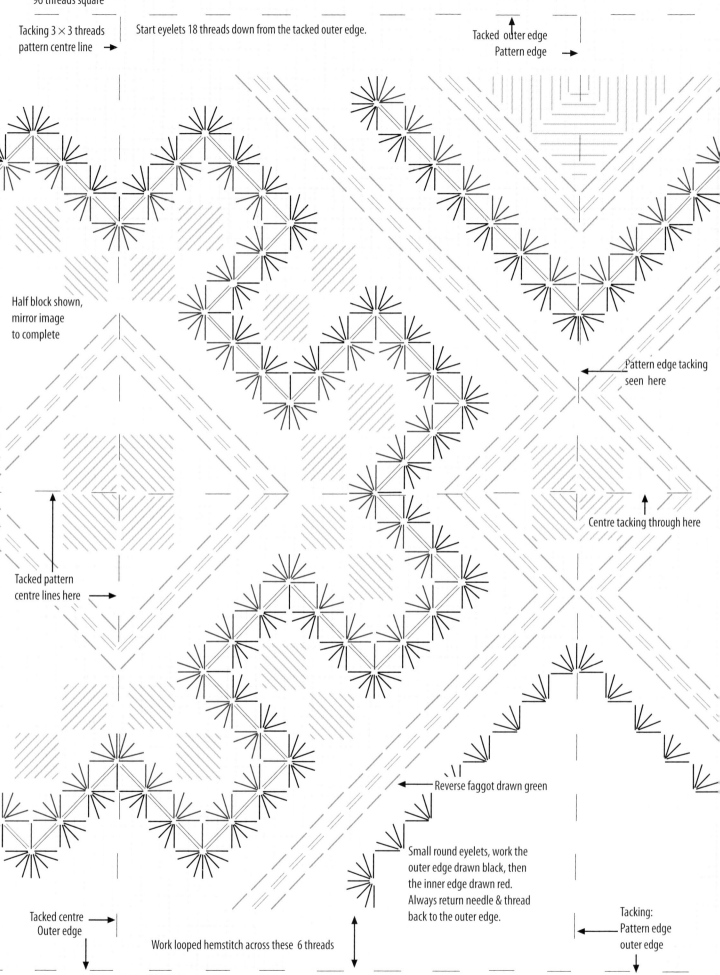

Half block shown,
mirror image
to complete

Tacked pattern
centre lines here ➡

⬅ Pattern edge tacking
seen here

Centre tacking through here ⬆

⬅ Reverse faggot drawn green

Small round eyelets, work the
outer edge drawn black, then
the inner edge drawn red.
Always return needle & thread
back to the outer edge.

Tacked centre ➡
Outer edge

Work looped hemstitch across these 6 threads

Tacking:
Pattern edge ⬅
outer edge

Maria PATTERN

During World War II Maria and her husband met in a German labour camp that came under British occupation in May 1945. As the communists had taken over Ukraine they decided not to go back home and took the opportunity offered to go to Australia and get as far away from Europe as possible. As refugee immigrants they were on a two year contract with the Australian government to work where they were placed. Maria was given work as a live-in maid with a wealthy family in Newcastle. The Australian family were wonderful, they adopted Maria and her husband as part of their extended family. When Maria's twin daughters were born the 'Australian' grandfather rushed to the hospital to see the babies stating that he was the grandfather and demanding to see them. The nurses did not stop to wonder why he spoke perfect English and Maria and her husband had strong Eastern European accents. The twins' Australian grandmother even bought a new car especially to take Maria and the babies home. Today Maria and her family still enjoy being part of their Australian family.

The Maria pattern is shown as a square teacloth. The main pattern is 9 cm deep. It also includes drawn thread and narrow borders worked around both edges to give a 17 cm deep border. This pattern would make a handsome wide border worked in two adjoining rows down the centre of a refectory table cloth or table scarf. The linen shown is a 25 count cream Dublin, the threads D.M.C. perle cottons Nos. 8 and 12, shade 644. The finished size 95 cm square.

You will need:

- 25 count linen, 100 cm × 100 cm
- Perle cottons No. 8 (6 balls), perle cotton No. 12 (4 balls)
- Small round frame, tapestry and crewel needles
- Sharp pointed scissors, tacking threads

The stitches and threads used are:

- Satin stitch, looped hemstitch and needleweaving are worked with No. 8 perle cotton.
- Reverse faggot, small round eyelets and hemstitch with No. 12 perle cotton.

Instructions:

- Read the useful information on linen threads, tacking, etc., pages 17–21.
- Important to read Drawn thread borders pages 104–107 for information, photographs and instructions showing how to deal with withdrawn threads. The inner drawn thread borders are completed before the pattern can be stitched at the corners.
- Stitches, see pages 22–25.
- Hems, page 111. Woven corner fillings, page 110.

Preparation:

- Straighten the linen and secure the raw edges.
- Tack a grid over 3 × 3 threads. The pattern is a 96 × 96 thread block.
- The colour coded graph shows half of a 96 thread square block. To see the mirror image turn the page around.

To work the Maria pattern follow the graph. Start with the small round eyelets, work the outer row drawn black, then the inner portion drawn red. Reverse faggot stitch is drawn green, work the centre diamond 18 threads up

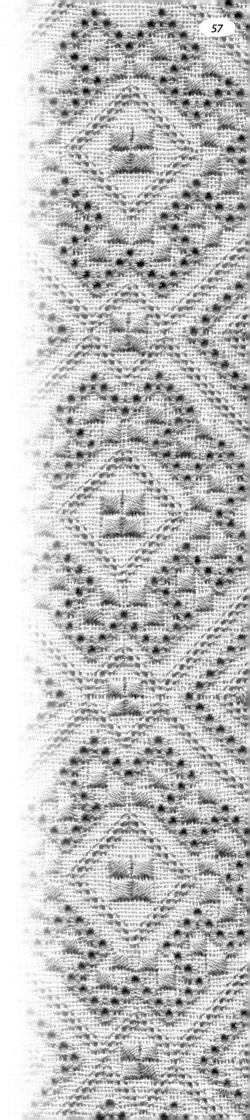

from the tacked pattern centre and the portion that links each block. Work the satin stitch drawn blue to complete the block.

Drawn thread borders are worked on both sides of the pattern and are edged with both looped hemstitch and plain hemstitch. Start the border at the centre tacking line and work towards each corner. If working this pattern as a tray cloth it will have a short inner border, see the working instructions for this, page 106, option 2 or 3.

From the centre of a long side the stitch sequence and borders to be worked are:

- For the 6 threads within the 96 thread block, see the graph. Leave 2 threads, cut 2, leave 2 and work looped hemstitch along the two withdrawn threads.

- A row of plain hemstitch is worked over the 3 × 3 threads beside the tacked edge.

- Cut 10 threads, they are not withdrawn until edged both sides with plain hemstitch. The border shown is No. 2, page 107.

- A row of plain hemstitch is worked over the next 3 × 3 threads

- Leave 2 threads, cut 2, leave 2 and work a second row of looped hemstitch.

- It is important to have each line of hemstitching gathering the same threads across the border into bundles of three ready for needleweaving.

- Once the withdrawn threads are hanging loose at the corners darn every second one back to the edge of the cloth. See pages 104–107 for instructions.

Woven corner filling. Complete the looped hemstitch, finish the threads off in the back of the work or carry them through the needle weaving tubes to strengthen the corner and support the woven corner filling. Use any No. 12 perle from the hemstitch to work the woven corner filling, see page 110 for working instructions and photographs.

Narrow Borders. Work the small patterns that border the needleweaving. Centre them on the tacking that marks the centre and the edge of each 96 thread pattern block and two threads out from the looped hemstitch, see graph No. 11, page 102.

Hem. Use the tacking to count the threads from the edge of the embroidery to where the edge of the hem will be. Mitre the corners and hemstitch over 3 × 3 threads. Use No. 12 perle, or threads withdrawn from the linen.

Work your name and date on the reverse side of the hem, not just initials. Use simple lettering that will be easily read in the future.

Congratulations! You have completed a beautiful piece of heritage embroidery that will become a family heirloom. Leaving such a beautiful example of your handiwork for future generations to enjoy will 'tell' family more about you than any bought objects.

Maria tacking grid and pattern layout

Tack 3 × 3 threads, pattern blocks 96 × 96 threads square.
Quarter of 100 cm square cloth shown.

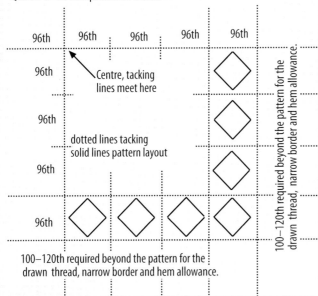

100–120th required beyond the pattern for the drawn thread, narrow border and hem allowance.

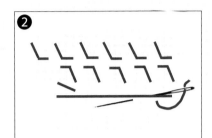

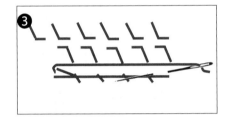

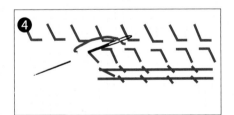

To work Merezhka Poltavska read the instructions over. Two threads are withdrawn and the first row of plain hemstitch is worked across the border from left to right, over two horizontal threads to gather three withdrawn threads together into bundles. Begin and finish three threads within the tacked hemstitch line.

1. Turn the work, for the second and following rows to be worked from right to left. Withdraw a second pair of threads as diagram shows, follow the pattern graph, stitch diagrams and work the number of hemstitches as graph lines show between an oval shape intersection. See the photograph.

2. For the first layering wrap the thread down and around the three thread bundles to be at the lower edge. Lay the working thread over the withdrawn linen threads and for the first layering of a row include the three threads at the hemline. (See the photograph, page 59.) Take the needle to the back of the work and bring it up below the layered thread and between the first three thread bundle. Hold it in place with a couched stitch. Continue in this manner until the intersection shown on the pattern is reached.

3. Repeat a second time as before, but this time the thread layered will be above the first and next to the hemstitch and will not need to be wrapped down and around the three thread bundle. The thread is now back to where the last hemstitch was worked and ready to work the next group of hemstitches and thread layering.

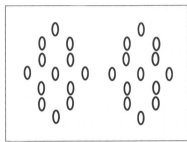

4. Continue in this way until the first row is completed and the last layering gathers in the three threads at the left hand hem edge.

Work the following rows as the graph shows and in the same manner as the second row.

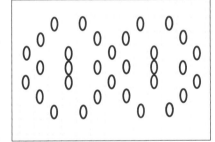

Only cut and withdraw threads once the previous row has been completed.

The final row is plain hemstitch like the first row. This edges the border with ladder hemstitch.

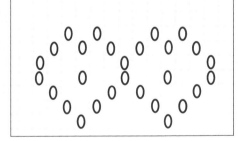

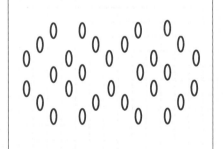

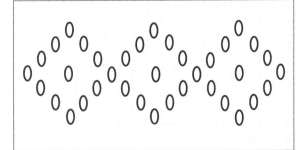

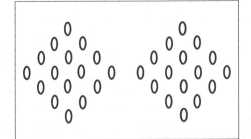

Merezhka Poltavska

Merezhka Poltavska is a Ukrainian drawn thread technique that is characterised by the method of working and is very similar to Bokara couching. Instead of stitching over a solid ground fabric, the working thread is laid across withdrawn threads and is held in place between the bundles of three fabric threads with tiny surmounting stitches. This is known as layering. It is a very beautiful, highly decorative and useful way of working drawn thread borders. It was used extensively in embroidery for the church, on the end of linen towels, as a band of 'lace' worked around the sleeves of men's and women's shirts and for household linen. It was generally worked with a self coloured thread to achieve the look of lace. Though this technique resembles lace, lace was rarely used by Ukrainian needlewomen on embroideries of any kind. Merezhka Poltavska provides a very secure, highly decorative border that can be further embellished by working narrow borders to edge it.

Merezhka is the name given to every style of Ukrainian cut and drawn work, from the simplest hemstitch through all their many forms of needleweaving, wrapping and layering. Poltavska indicates that it is the method of working this technique known in Poltava, East Ukraine, the region where most of that country's whitework comes from.

The linen shown is 25 count Dublin, colour cream. The threads are D.M.C. perle cottons Nos. 8 and 12, shade ecru. The finished size of each table mat is 44 cm × 30 cm .

You will need:

- 25 count linen, 35 cm × 50 cm for each table mat
- Perle cottons No. 8 and No. 12
- Small round frame, tapestry needles
- Small sharp pointed scissors, tacking threads

The stitches and threads are:

- Layering and narrow borders are worked with No 8 perle cotton.
- Hem with No. 12 perle cotton, the instructions are on page 111.

Preparation:

- Read the useful information on linen threads, tacking, etc., pages 17–21.
- Straighten the linen and secure the raw edges.
- Tack over 3 × 3 threads 14 cm down the centre of the mat lengthways.
- Tack the hemstitch line, the hem edge and the turn under line for a 12 thread hem. Use the accurate centre tacking to count where to begin each tacking line as shown on the diagram.

Instructions:

To read the graphed patterns:

- Each horizontal graph line equals two threads.
- Each vertical graph line equals three threads.
- The oval shapes on the pattern diagrams show where the layering begins and finishes, this creates the square holes or intersections required for making the pattern. For other evenweave linens or fabrics the sequence of achieving the square hole could be different. Work a sample to check.
- Between each oval shape there will be three rows of stitching, plain hemstitch, plus two layerings. Traditionally a third row of layering was worked

but it would depend upon how lacy an effect is wanted and the type of linen and thread used.

- Plain hemstitch is worked the number of vertical lines that the pattern shows between each oval shape. This brings the thread to the place where it can be wrapped down and around the three-thread bundle to be in place for the first layering, see the diagrams. The second layering is above the first, see diagram 3.

- All threads are cut and withdrawn from the centre tacking line, only two are cut at a time, one withdrawn, the other darned into the weave.

- Each row of layering is completed before starting the following one.

- Layering is only worked in one direction from right to left.

- Because of the way the pattern is begun and finished, ladder hemstitch will edge the border.

- Merezhka Poltavska is worked across one short side only and out to within three threads of the hemstitch line, see the photograph.

To begin Merezhka Poltavska cut two threads beside the centre tacking line and seventeen threads down from the hemstitch line. Completely withdraw the first thread and withdraw the second one back to just three threads within the hemstitch line at each long side and darn it into the weave. Read Drawn thread information pages 104–107.

Work plain hemstitch across the border, begin at the left of a short side and 15 threads down from the hemstitch line as shown on the tacking diagram. Have the work in a small round frame and turn it so that the short end hemstitch line is close to you.

To begin the second and following rows, cut two threads, withdraw one and darn the other into the weave as before. Turn the mat and work from right to left. Follow the stitch and pattern diagrams. There are three rows of stitching between each oval shape, plain hemstitch and two rows of layering.

To start and finish perle cottons. Begin by darning the thread into the weave of the linen to work the hemstitch over. To finish, carry it under the hemstitch or hide it under the layering. See 'Starting and Finishing Threads,' page 18–19.

Narrow Borders. Select the borders of your choice, work them next to the ladder hemstitch, and both sides of the border. See pages 102–103.

Work your name and date on the reverse side of the hem.

Hems. Mitre the corners and work hemstitch over 3 × 3 threads with No. 12 perle cotton or similar, see page 111.

Congratulations! You have completed a beautiful set of table mats that will complement your best table setting. If each mat is worked with different patterns they will create much interest and add to your stitching pleasure.

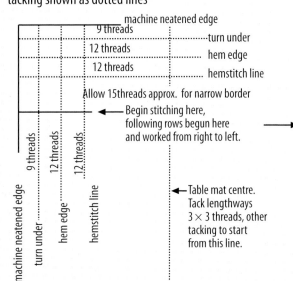

Merezhka Poltavska table mats tacking diagram

Half only shown. Tack 3 × 3 threads 14 cm down the centre, tacking shown as dotted lines

machine neatened edge
9 threads .... turn under
12 threads .... hem edge
12 threads .... hemstitch line
Allow 15 threads approx. for narrow border
← Begin stitching here, following rows begun here and worked from right to left.

machine neatened edge | 9 threads | turn under | 12 threads | hem edge | 12 threads | hemstitch line

← Table mat centre. Tack lengthways 3 × 3 threads, other tacking to start from this line.

Mychajlo Pattern

Each graph line equals one thread.
Tacking over 4 × 4 threads, drawn black

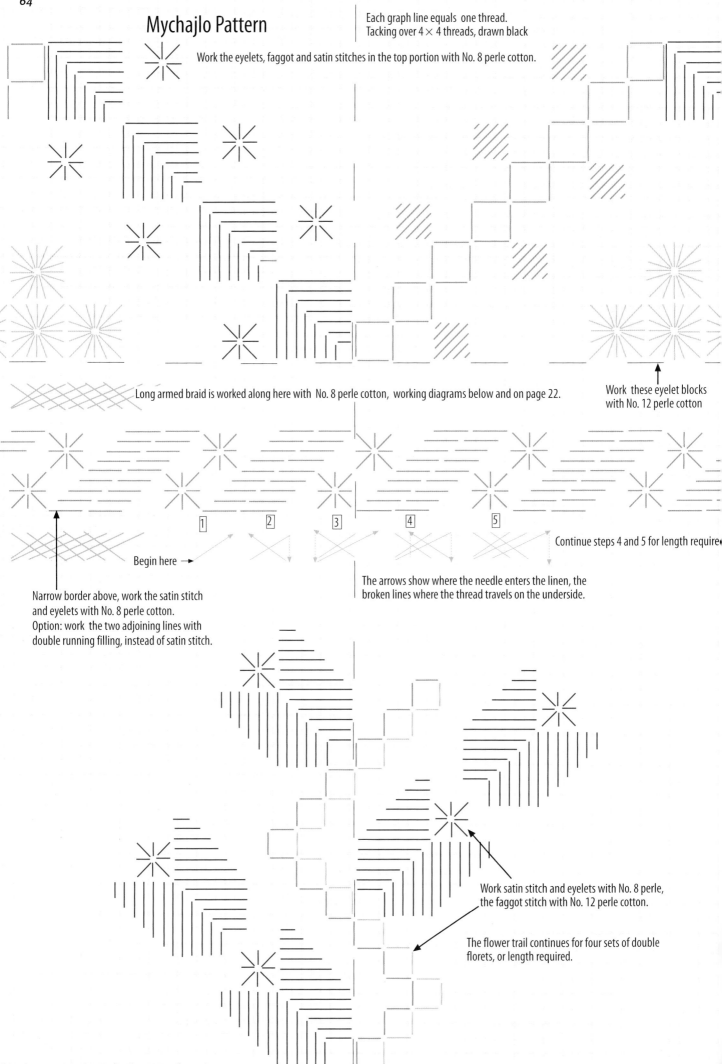

Work the eyelets, faggot and satin stitches in the top portion with No. 8 perle cotton.

Work these eyelet blocks
with No. 12 perle cotton

Long armed braid is worked along here with No. 8 perle cotton, working diagrams below and on page 22.

1 2 3 4 5

Continue steps 4 and 5 for length require●

Begin here →

The arrows show where the needle enters the linen, the
broken lines where the thread travels on the underside.

Narrow border above, work the satin stitch
and eyelets with No. 8 perle cotton.
Option: work the two adjoining lines with
double running filling, instead of satin stitch.

Work satin stitch and eyelets with No. 8 perle,
the faggot stitch with No. 12 perle cotton.

The flower trail continues for four sets of double
florets, or length required.

 *Mychajlo* PATTERN

During the early years of World War II German forces governed, and in spite of the many interruptions during those troubled times, Mychajlo (Mekhaylo) managed with the help of his parents to complete his high school education. With the German resistance broken and the rapid advances of Soviet forces to regain Western Ukraine, Mychajlo simply left home and eventually joined many others in a West German displaced persons' camp. In 1949 he took the Australian government's offer to relocate to the other side of the world. Once settled in Australia Mychajlo was able to complete the tertiary studies begun in Germany and worked as a microscopist for the same company for 30 years. As well as working full time, and on his retirement, he has had a long involvement with the Ukrainian Arts and Crafts Museum and used his photographic skills to record each of the 6000 items housed, plus undertaking many of the other tasks required. This extensive collection of Ukrainian artefacts will ensure that future generations do not forget their rich culture. It is also a valuable asset to Australia's wealth of cultural mix.

The Mychajlo pattern is shown as a runner with a trail of floral motifs descending from a 4.5 cm deep border worked across each end. This style of pattern is a feature of Ukrainian needlework and seen in books published in that country. The finished size is 91 cm × 25 cm. The linen shown is Glenshee 28 thread count, the threads are D.M.C. perle cottons Nos. 8 and 12, shade 927.

You will need:

- 28 count linen, 90 cm × 30 cm or 36" × 12"
- Perle cottons No. 8 and No. 12
- Small round frame
- Tapestry and crewel needles
- Tacking threads

The stitches and threads used are:

- Satin, double running filling, square eyelets, long arm braid and faggot stitch along the top border are all worked with No. 8 perle cotton.
- The trailing faggot stitch, groups of square eyelets and hemstitch are worked with No. 12 perle cotton.

Instructions:

- Read the useful information on linen threads, tacking, etc., pages 17–21.
- Stitches see pages 22–25.
- Tack a grid 4 × 4 threads. It ensures accuracy and is a simple method for pattern placement.
- Hems, page 111.

Preparation:

- Straighten the linen and secure the raw edges.
- Follow the tacking grid and pattern layout, drawn full width. It shows where it is placed.
- Tack a line 4 × 4 threads down the centre of the runner; use this as a guide to tack the hem lines and for pattern placement.
- The four centre long tacking lines are 64 threads apart from each other, the two outer lines are 32 threads from their neighbour. The border is 32 threads deep and 42 threads down from the hem edge.

To work the Mychajlo pattern use the colour coded graph; it shows only a portion of the pattern and includes the tacking shown as fine black lines.

Begin at the top border beside the tacked line and work the faggot stitch and satin stitch blocks in a continuous line one side at a time. When coming to a satin stitch block take the needle four threads out from the faggot stitch and work the small block in towards the line of faggot stitching. Continue in this way.

The other portions of the top border are blocks of satin stitch. They are also worked in a continuous line up one side and down the other. Work the eyelets as the stitching proceeds. Continue alternating between the faggot and satin stitch until the top border is completed.

- See the graph where the faggot and satin stitch portions meet, they share the same space.

Groups of square eyelets are worked at the centre of each 64 thread block and on the lower tacked line.

Long armed braid stitch is worked across the runner and within the outer tacking lines. The first line is two threads down from the tacking and is three threads deep. A second line is worked twelve threads down from the first. If a thinner line is preferred use No. 12 perle cotton. The working instructions are on the graphed pattern and page 22.

The narrow border is eight threads deep and two threads from the long armed braid stitch. Either work the two adjoining lines as diagonal satin stitches or as double running filling stitch. The photograph shows them worked as double running filling stitch. The working instructions are on page 22. The small square eyelets are worked between the border as it proceeds.

The floral trails can be as long or short as required. Begin faggot stitch 12 threads down from the long armed braid. Cut a thread twice as long as required, leave half the length of thread as a long tail parked ready to work the second line of stitching. This method avoids having extra threads to finish off in the back of the work. Work the trail to length required.

Both the florets and small eyelet centres are worked with the same thread, note where placed on the graph.

Hem. Tack the 3 lines required. Mitre the corners and work hemstitch over 3 × 3 threads.

Work your name and date on the reverse side of the hem in a simple back stitch.

There are a number of options for using this lovely pattern. It would work well as an antimacassar, or work the top portion down the centre of a refectory table cloth and have the floral trails descending from both sides of it.

Well done! You have completed a lovely piece of Ukrainian Whitework that will enhance any piece of furniture.

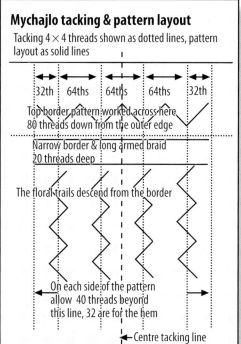

Mychajlo tacking & pattern layout

Tacking 4 × 4 threads shown as dotted lines, pattern layout as solid lines

32th   64ths   64ths   64ths   32th

Top border pattern worked across here 80 threads down from the outer edge

Narrow border & long armed braid 20 threads deep

The floral trails descend from the border

On each side of the pattern allow 40 threads beyond this line, 32 are for the hem

← Centre tacking line

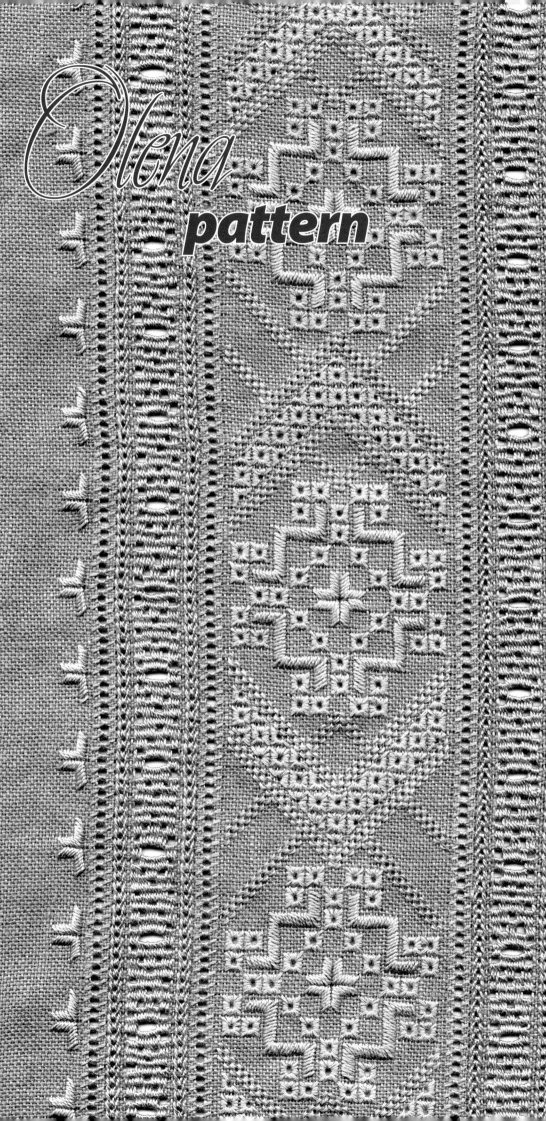

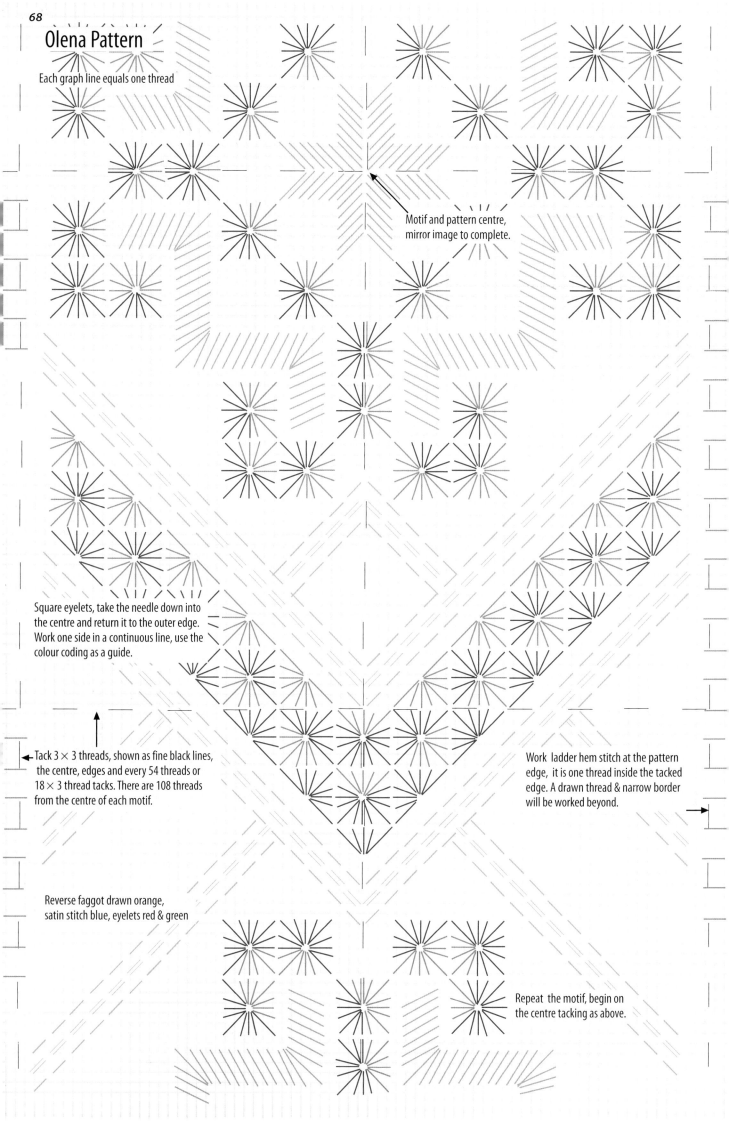

Olena Pattern

Each graph line equals one thread

Motif and pattern centre,
mirror image to complete.

Square eyelets, take the needle down into
the centre and return it to the outer edge.
Work one side in a continuous line, use the
colour coding as a guide.

← Tack 3 × 3 threads, shown as fine black lines,
the centre, edges and every 54 threads or
18 × 3 thread tacks. There are 108 threads
from the centre of each motif.

Work ladder hem stitch at the pattern
edge, it is one thread inside the tacked
edge. A drawn thread & narrow border
will be worked beyond.

Reverse faggot drawn orange,
satin stitch blue, eyelets red & green

Repeat the motif, begin on
the centre tacking as above.

 *Olena* PATTERN

Olena's grandparents were farmers and sold their meat and eggs at the local market. In 1950 the Soviet authorities seized the farm that their family had owned for many generations, and deported them and their four small children to Siberia to serve eighteen years' hard labour. They were given just twenty-four hours to pack a few belongings to take with them. Once in Siberia, the family lived in one small room in barracks that housed many others. In spite of the hard work and other difficulties, Olena's grandmother's spirit was never broken, she made sure that the children went to school and were able to get a good education. She was a superb cook and the family always celebrated all the feast days of the Ukrainian Orthodox church with some of her wonderful cooking. In 1968 they were finally able to return to Ukraine — not to their own home but to a one room flat. Olena has wonderful treasured memories of her grandmother as an 'iron lady' and a splendid cook.

The Olena pattern is shown as an antimacassar, a useful, decorative protection to place on the back of an upholstered chair. The linen used is Cashel 28 thread count, shade Amsterdam blue. The threads are D.M.C. perle No. 8 and stranded cotton both shade 926. The finished size is 65 cm × 38 cm.

You will need:

- 28 count linen, 50 cm × 70 cm or length required
- Perle 8 and stranded cottons. See thread options, page 18
- Small round frame, tapestry and crewel needles
- Small sharp pointed scissors, tacking threads

The stitches and threads used are:

- Satin stitch, needle weaving and looped hemstitch are worked with No. 8 perle cotton.
- The square eyelets, reverse faggot and ladder hemstitch with two strands of stranded cotton.
- The hem is stitched with threads withdrawn from the linen.

Instructions:

- Read the useful information on linen threads, tacking, etc., pages 17–21.
- Stitches, pages 22–25.
- Before proceeding read Drawn thread borders, pages 104–107, for information and instructions showing how to deal with withdrawn threads.
- Hems, page 111.

Preparation:

- Straighten the linen and secure the raw edges.
- Tack a grid over 3 × 3 threads. It ensures accuracy and is a simple method for pattern placement.
- The Olena pattern is 72 threads deep and 108 threads from the centre of each motif.
- Tack the centre first, then the hem edge, stitch line and turn under. Use this accurate tacking to place the other lines.

To work the Olena pattern use the colour coded graph, it includes the tacking shown as fine black lines. Begin by stitching the square eyelets, start at

the centre of the cloth and 10 cm or 112 threads from the edge of the linen. The eyelets are colour coded to show that each side is worked separately in a continuous line. Use this as a guide only and not the only route to take.

- Satin stitch is worked over four threads, note the change of direction and the stitch placement at each turn.
- Reverse faggot stitch is worked in two adjoining rows and over two fabric threads.

Drawn thread border. For a single sided border begin both the ladder and looped hemstitched rows at the tacking that marks the hemstitch line, right hand side of the border and work across to the tacked line at the left side. This allows the stitching to lay in the same direction. Note that the ladder hemstitch is one thread inside the tacked pattern edge, see the graph. The stitch sequence is:

- Leave 3 threads, cut and withdraw two, leave 3 and work ladder hemstitch across these 8 threads.
- Leave 1 thread, cut and withdraw 2, leave 3 and work looped hemstitch along the two withdrawn threads, each stitch is three threads long.
- Cut twelve threads. They are not withdrawn until the hemstitches are completed. The needle woven border worked here is No. 4, page 108.
- Leave 3 threads, cut 2, leave 1 and work a second line of looped hemstitch.
- Leave 3 threads, cut 2, leave 3 and work a second line of ladder hemstitch across these 8 threads.
- It is important to have the various hemstitches gathering the same threads across the border into bundles of three ready for needle weaving.
- Once the threads have been withdrawn back to within three threads of the hemstitch line, darn every second one back to the edge of the linen.
- Read For Single sided borders. This gives information on how to avoid the ugly gap between the linen and needle woven border, see page 107.

Needle weaving is begun at the pattern centre line and worked out to each side. Only withdraw approximately 5–6 cm of thread at a time.

Narrow border. The motif shown is one side of the satin stitch centre of the Olena pattern. It is positioned on the same line as the oval shape in the needle weaving pattern and one thread out from the ladder hemstitch.

Olena tacking grid and pattern layout width shown.
Tack 3 × 3 threads, shown as dotted line, pattern layout solid line, pattern depth 72 threads.

pattern centre line

Drawn thread borders worked across here

| 78th | 54th | 54th | 54th | 54th | 78th |

48 th hem allowance

48 th hem allowance

Drawn thread borders worked across here

Allow 112 threads for the drawn thread borders and hem

Hem will be stitched three threads from the edge of the needle woven border. For an 18 thread deep hem, allow 45 threads, the extra three threads listed on the tacking diagram are those used to link the drawn thread borders to the linen.

Mitre the corners and work hemstitch over 3 × 3 threads.

Work your name and date and any other information on the reverse side of the hem in a simple back stitch.

Well done! You have completed a lovely piece of Ukrainian Whitework that will enhance any living room.

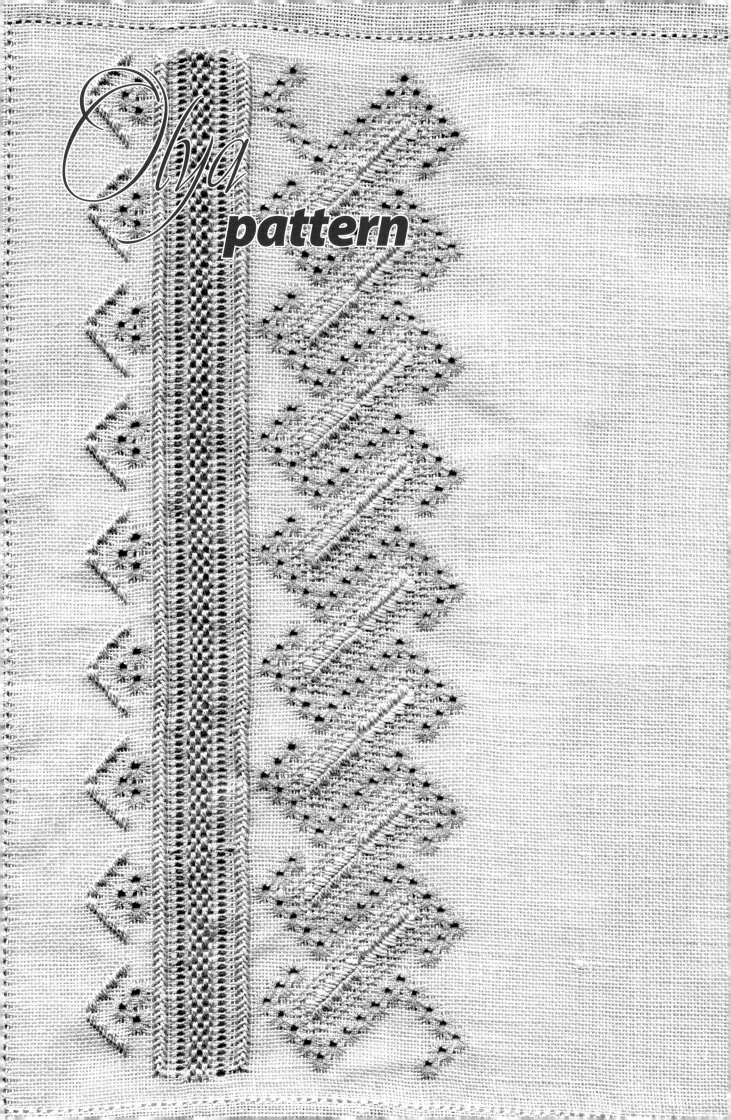

Olya Pattern

The 4 × 4 thread tacking is shown as fine black lines and shows the pattern placement.

Each graph line equals one thread.

Link each motif widthways as above. First work the large round eyelets drawn red in a continuous line to establish the pattern, then the second row drawn green. Always return the needle and thread back to the outer edge. Satin stitch is drawn blue. Reverse faggot stitch is orange, note that it changes direction on a cross stitch.

Narrow Border motif, see the photograph. They are each placed above the top eyelet and beyond the long armed braid and drawn thread border. There are four threads between each motif.

Olya pattern option 2.
Work the motifs lengthways as a narrow border, see the lavender bag page 99.

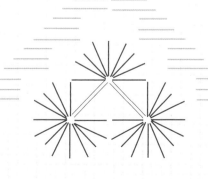

Olya PATTERN

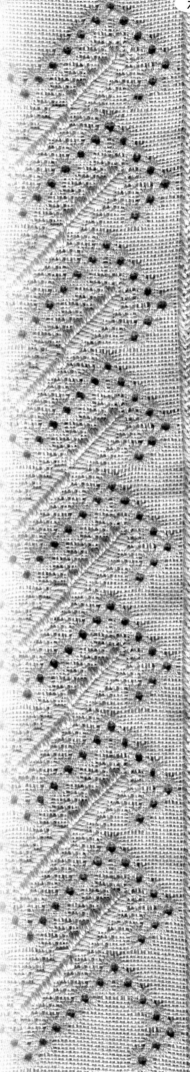

Olya's husband was an active member of the Ukrainian Insurgent Army (UPA). During a major confrontation between the KGB units and the UPA, he fell into their hands on the Ukrainian Christmas Day, January 7th 1948. He was brutally tortured and his body left lying in an open field as a warning to others not to join or support the UPA. Fearing persecution, Olya left her baby son with her parents and fled to a remote part of the country. Eventually she remarried and took her son, aged four, to her new home. Ironically, the boy grew up to serve as a colonel in the Red Russian army and managed an early warning radar station. He died young due to prolonged exposure to high frequency radiation.

The Olya pattern is shown as a runner with a border at each end. This style of pattern where the motif changes direction sharply is a feature of much Ukrainian needlework. The drawn thread border would also seem to be unique to Ukraine. The Olya pattern could be worked as a long narrow border with one motif following on from the next, as shown on the graph. This pattern would be ideal for lavender bags and bookmarks, see option 2 on the graph.

The linen shown is 30 count Semco Willow grey, the threads are Anchor perle cottons No. 8 and stranded cotton, both shade 858, plus a reel of Coats Duet sewing cotton shade 216. The finished size is 29 cm × 66 cm.

You will need:

- 30 count linen, 35 cm × 70 cm
- Perle cotton No. 8 and both stranded and sewing cotton
- Small round frame
- Tapestry and crewel needles
- Small sharp pointed scissors
- Tacking threads

The stitches and threads used are:

- Satin stitch, long armed braid, verkhoploot narrow border and needle-woven border are all worked with No. 8 perle cotton.
- Large round eyelets with a single length of Coats Duet sewing cotton.
- Reverse faggot stitch and ladder hemstitch with two strands of stranded cotton.
- Hemstitch with threads withdrawn from the linen.

Instructions:

- Read the useful information on linen threads, tacking, etc., pages 17–21.
- Before proceeding read Drawn thread borders, pages 104–107, for information and instructions showing how to deal with withdrawn threads.
- Stitch diagrams, see pages 22–25.
- Hems, page 111.

Preparation:

- Straighten the linen and secure the raw edges, see page 17.
- Tack down the centre length of the runner over four × four threads, then the edge of the hem on the short side. Use this accurate tacking to place the other tacked lines that mark each block.
- Begin the main border 100 threads down from the edge of the linen or as your preference.

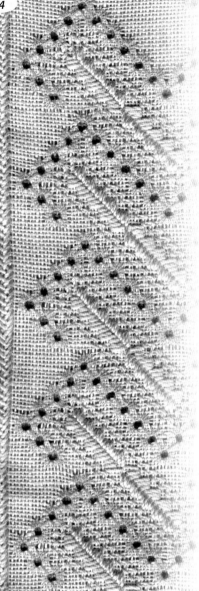

To work the Olya pattern use the colour coded graph; it includes the tacking shown as fine black lines. Each pattern block is 64 threads deep × 32 threads wide and is worked at both ends of the runner. See the pattern layout and tacking grid.

Begin by working the large round eyelets to establish the pattern, use the accurate tacking to place the pattern within each tacked block. The large round eyelets are colour coded and worked in a continuous line.

Follow the graph to place the satin stitch drawn blue, note that it flows into the next block.

Reverse faggot stitch surrounds the satin stitch, it is drawn orange. Note that it changes direction at each end on a cross stitch.

Long armed braid borders the main pattern. It is four threads deep, not the three shown on the stitch diagram, page 22.

Drawn thread border is worked one thread out from the Long armed braid and is most possibly unique to Ukraine. It is border No. 7, page 108. The stitch sequence is: one thread out from the long armed braid.

- Leave two threads, cut two, leave two and work ladder hemstitch over 2 × 2 threads and across the six threads.

- Cut six threads; these are not withdrawn until edged both sides with ladder hemstitch. Once the six threads are withdrawn Merezhka Verkhoploot will be worked across them from right to left.

- Leave two threads, cut two, leave two and work ladder hemstitch over 2 × 2 threads and across the six threads.

A narrow border of motifs. Both eyelets and satin stitch are worked at the outer edge of the pattern. The diagram is included with the pattern graph. These small motifs are placed above the top eyelet, main border and are four threads apart from each other, see the photograph.

Hem. Count the threads from edge of the border out to hem, tack to mark the lines required for a 12 thread deep hem. Mitre the corners and work hemstitch over 3 × 3 threads with threads withdrawn from the linen.

Work your name and date on the reverse side of the hem in a simple back stitch.

Well done! You have completed a lovely piece of Ukrainian Whitework that would make an ideal gift for someone special and would be admired and enjoyed for many years.

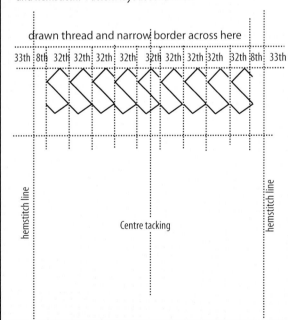

Olya tacking grid and pattern layout
One end of a 35 cm × 70 cm runner shown
Tack 4 × 4 threads, shown as dotted lines, 32 threads between each pattern & 8 threads between the pattern and hemstitch. Pattern layout solid lines.

drawn thread and narrow border across here

33th | 8th | 32th | 32th | 32th | 32th | 32th | 32th | 32th | 32th | 32th | 8th | 33th

hemstitch line

Centre tacking

hemstitch line

Orion
pattern

Orion Pattern

Graph one

Each graph line equals one thread.
Tack a 3 × 3 thread grid.

Orion pattern is 36 threads
wide and 96 threads between
the centre tacking of each
graph.

The reverse faggot stitch drawn
orange is over two threads and
worked with No. 12 perle cotton.
The satin stitch drawn blue is over
four and across two threads and
worked with No. 8 perle cotton.

Tacking over 3 × 3 threads.
Note the eyelets are
always worked within the
three thread tacking.

A band of eyelets like this
is worked at the top of the
pattern, but slanted in the
opposite direction, see
graph 2.

Link graph two here to
continue the Orion
pattern.

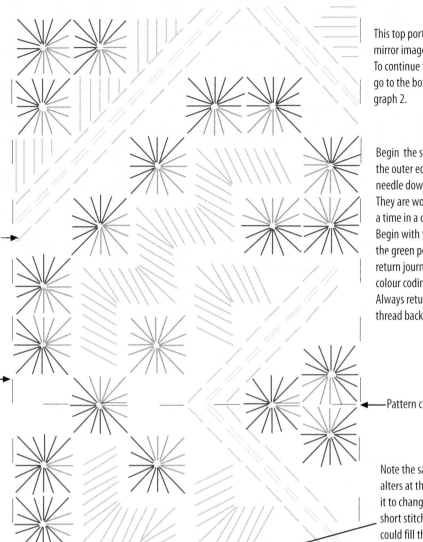

This top portion is a
mirror image of below.
To continue the pattern
go to the bottom of
graph 2.

Begin the square eyelets at
the outer edge and take the
needle down into the centre.
They are worked one side at
a time in a continuous line.
Begin with the red and work
the green portion on the
return journey. Use this
colour coding as a guide only.
Always return the needle and
thread back to the outer edge.

Pattern centre tack this line.

Note the satin stitch count
alters at the corners to allow
it to change direction. If preferred
short stitches over two threads
could fill these gaps. They are
shown drawn at this place only.

Originally these bands were worked
freely without a thread count on
hand spun closely woven linens.
To make the eyelets the crossed
warp and weft threads at the centre
of an eyelet were cut then it was
firmly bound with close satin stitch.

Tacking over 3 × 3 threads
aids accuracy.
Note the eyelets are always
beside the three thread tacks.

Orion Pattern
Graph two

Link graph one here

Each graph line equals
one thread.

Tacking over 3 × 3 threads.
Note the eyelets are
always worked within
the three thread tacking.

Pattern centre tack this line

Two or three straight bands
of this style of whitework
pattern were worked around
the upper sleeves of shirts.
The outer edges often
finished with a narrow satin
stitch border. The hem edge
and other openings may
have been neatened with a
narrow Merezkha drawn
thread border. The neck and
cuffs were often gathered or
smocked to hold the shape.

Orion pattern is 36 threads
wide and 96 threads between
the centre of graph one and
graph two.

Note the satin stitch count
changes at the corners,it is
not as obvious once worked.

To complete the table scarf
edge this pattern with ladder
hemstitch and finish with
a narrow border. To work
ladder hemstitch, see page 105.

To continue the pattern
this portion links with the
top of graph one. Repeat
until the required length
is achieved.

Photographs: Michael Hanytsky, from the Ukrainian Arts and Crafts Museum, Melbourne.

Inset: Enlargement of a second shirt in their collection.

Orion PATTERN

As a young man growing up in Ukraine, Orion studied architecture. With the retreat of the Germans and advancement of the Red Army to retake Ukraine he was able to make his way to West Germany. He was living in a displaced persons' camp in the British sector when peace was declared in May 1945. Along with 21 000 other Ukrainians, Orion chose to take the Australian government's offer to settle in that country. After completing the compulsory two years contracted work, Orion was able to find employment in an architectural firm. When the Ukrainian Catholics living in Melbourne decided it was time to build a cathedral church, Orion was delighted. He was asked to prepare the original sketches and was able to advise and co-ordinate with the architect the congregation's requirements. A Ukrainian Arts and Crafts Museum was built alongside the cathedral to house the many significant items that were being collected to ensure that future generations of Ukrainian / Australians would not forget their culture or their roots. Orion was appointed its manager and continued in this honorary position for 20 years. He introduced a cataloguing system to itemise the many items in the collection and undertook many other tasks required for such a venture.

The Orion pattern is shown as a table scarf designed to place along the centre of a plain easy care linen look table cloth to dress it up. It has two, three and four thread stitch units and does not finish with a straight edge at each end. This count change is a feature of Ukrainian Whitework and gives it a special charm and beauty. This style of whitework was worked on closely woven linen around the upper sleeve of shirts. To work eyelets threads had to be cut, then the hole made was firmly stitched around. The Orion pattern has been developed from a photograph of an embroidered shirt sleeve that would have been worn for festive occasions.

The linen shown is 25 count Lauder, shade Old White. It was purchased many years ago. The threads are D.M.C. perle cottons Nos. 8 and 12, shade Blanc Neige. The finished size is 105 cm × 17 cm.

You will need:

- 25 count linen, 110 cm × 2 cm
- Perle cottons Nos. 8 and 12
- Small round frame
- Tapestry and crewel needles
- Small sharp pointed scissors
- Tacking threads

The stitches and threads used are:

- Satin stitch and ladder hemstitch are worked with No. 8 perle cotton.
- Reverse faggot, square eyelets and the hem with No. 12 perle or similar, see page 18 for options.

Instructions:

- Read the useful information on linen threads, tacking, etc., pages 17–21.
- For stitches see pages 22–25.
- Hems, pages 111.
- Narrow borders, page 102–103.

Preparation:

- Straighten the linen and secure the raw edges.

- Tack an accurate grid 3 × 3 threads. Follow the tacking grid and pattern layout.
- The Orion pattern is 36 threads wide and 96 threads from the centre of each pattern.
- Tack down the centre first, next the outer edges then the centre of each motif as shown.

To work the Orion pattern use the colour coded graph. It includes the tacking shown as fine black lines. Begin stitching the square eyelets at the centre of the cloth and follow the graph to establish the pattern. Note that they are colour coded to show that each side is worked separately in a continuous line. The colour coding is a guide only and not the only route to take when stitching them.

The reverse faggot is worked in two adjoining rows over two fabric threads.

Satin stitch is worked over four threads. Note the change of direction and the stitch placement at each turn. If the gap at the change of direction shows work extra short stitches over two threads at the corners, see the graph for where to place them.

Diagonal bands option. Instead of working the straight satin stitches between the reverse faggot and square eyelets, work half a square eyelet to fill that space. This would give a very lacy effect.

Ladder hemstitch. From the pattern edge leave one thread, see the photograph.

- Leave 3 threads, cut and withdraw 2 threads, leave 3 threads and work ladder hemstitch across these 8 threads.
- Once the withdrawn threads are hanging loose at the corners, darn every second one back to the edge of the cloth, see pages 104–107 for instructions.

Narrow border. Motifs are worked along the outer edge and one thread out from the ladder hemstitch. Position them at the centre of each block with two further motifs between. As for other Ukrainian Whitework patterns there is a thread count difference, some of these small motifs will be 33 threads from centre to centre and others will be 30. See border No. 4, page 102.

Hem. Count the threads from the edge of the border out to hem, tack to mark the lines required. Mitre the corners and work hemstitch over 3 × 3 threads.

Work your name and date and any other information on the reverse side of the hem in a simple back stitch.

Well done! You have completed a lovely piece of Ukrainian Whitework that will enhance any table setting and make an every day table cloth look special and suitable for any occasion.

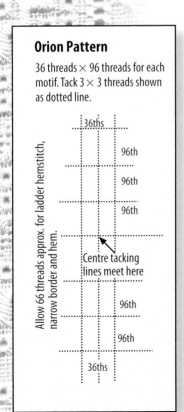

Orion Pattern

36 threads × 96 threads for each motif. Tack 3 × 3 threads shown as dotted line.

Pattern Darning

Pattern Darning

Each graph line equals one thread

Always start Pattern Darning where the horizontal fabric thread lays over the vertical, or the warp thread is over the weft.

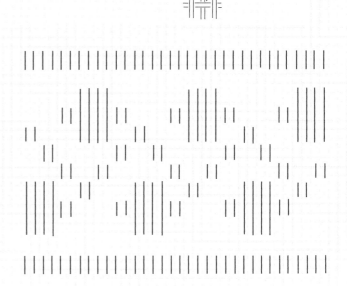

Start here

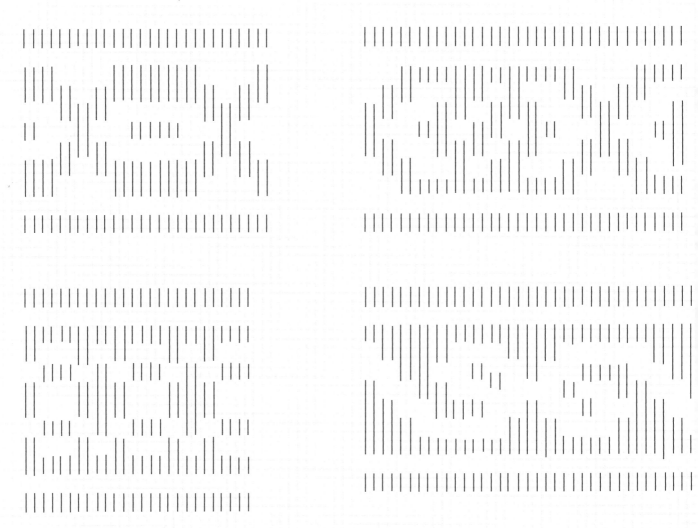

The arrows show where the needle enters the linen, the dotted lines are the threads on the underside. Once the first row is completed turn and work the second line, then turn and work down the following line. Continue in this way until completed.

To finish at the same place each side of a border, begin the pattern beside the centre tacking line.

Pattern Darning

Pattern darning is one of the earliest styles of needlework known. Generally it is worked across the length of the border from right to left and the pattern is not complete until the last row is worked. In Ukraine and New Zealand pattern darning is also worked up and down the depth to quickly establish a pattern that is repeated for the required length. Ukrainians work on the reverse side of the fabric, their stitch sequence changes each row and many of their patterns are deeper than ours and often include a stepped edging. For Ukrainian Pattern darning see the Needlework books listed on page 112.

The patterns illustrated were developed in Dunedin by the late Miss Helen M. Moran sometime between 1930 and 1940. She considered the technique ideal for school children as the pattern grew quickly, they were simple to work and encouraged young teenagers to enjoy needlework. For that reason Miss Moran's patterns have been used rather than the deeper more complex Ukrainian patterns. The project has been given a Ukrainian look with the addition of drawn thread ladder hemstitch and narrow borders to edge the pattern darning. This simple needlework technique would provide a good family project for winter months and can be used without the drawn thread and narrow borders.

The linen shown is 25 count soft green purchased many years ago. The threads are D.M.C. perle cotton No. 8 shade 926. The finished size of each table mat is 30 cm × 44 cm.

You will need:

- 25 count linen, 36 cm × 50 cm for each mat, plus an extra piece for hemstitching
- Perle cotton No. 8
- Small round frame
- Tapestry needles
- Small sharp pointed scissors
- Tacking threads

The stitches and threads used are:

- Pattern darning, ladder hemstitch and satin stitch with No. 8 perle cotton.
- Hemstitch with threads withdrawn from the linen.

Instructions:

- Read the useful information on linen, threads, tacking, etc., pages 17–21.
- Before proceeding read Drawn thread borders, pages 104–107, for information, photographs and instructions on how to work these borders and deal with withdrawn threads.
- Narrow borders, see pages 102–103.
- Ladder hemstitch, page 105.
- Hems, page 111.

Preparation:

- Straighten the linen and secure the raw edges, see page 17.
- The embroidery is worked across one short side only and out to the hemstitch line at both sides of the mat.
- Tack accurately over 4 × 4 threads, 14 cm down the centre of the mat lengthways. Use this accurate centre tacking to place the hem edge line.

- Tack the hem edge line over 4 × 4 threads, use this as a guide for tacking the turn under and hemstitch lines on the other three sides shown on the diagram.

It is important to begin pattern darning where the horizontal fabric thread lays over the vertical or in other terms the warp thread is over the weft. Beginning at this place ensures that the working thread is linked around the weave and does not slip down a vertical thread to the space below. See the diagram on the pattern graph.

Begin pattern darning at the centre of a short side and 20 threads down from the hemstitch line. Work out to the tacked hemstitch line on a long side. Start back at the centre again and work out in the opposite direction to the hemstitch line.

- The arrows drawn on the graph show the method of working pattern darning. Once the first row has been worked turn and work back to the top edge. Continue like this turning at the end of each row until the border is completed.

- On the reverse side pattern darning gives a negative pattern to the front of the work. These negative patterns can also be used as positives.

- The threads can be finished off on the reverse side under the two thread border at the pattern edge.

Drawn thread

- Ladder hemstitch is worked both sides of the pattern darning and one thread out from it.

- Start at the centre of the cloth. Leave three threads, cut two threads, leave two threads.

- Work ladder hemstitch over two × two threads and across six, this leaves the one thread next to the pattern darning unstitched.

Once the withdrawn threads are hanging loose at the corners, darn every second one back to the edge of the cloth, see pages 104–107 for instructions.

Narrow Borders. Select the borders of your choice, they are worked one thread out from the ladder hemstitch.

Hem. Mitre the corners and work hemstitch over 2 × 2 threads around the embroidered portion of the table mat only, then over four × four threads to complete the hem. Use threads withdrawn from the spare piece of linen to give a good match.

Work your name and date on the reverse side of the hem.

Congratulations! You have completed a beautiful set of table mats that will enhance any dining table and if each is worked with different patterns they will create much interest.

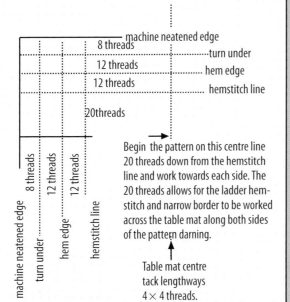

Pattern Darning table mats tacking diagram

Tack 4 × 4 threads 14 cm down the centre, tacking shown as dotted lines.

machine neatened edge
8 threads — turn under
12 threads — hem edge
12 threads — hemstitch line
20 threads

machine neatened edge / 8 threads turn under / 12 threads hem edge / 12 threads hemstitch line

Begin the pattern on this centre line 20 threads down from the hemstitch line and work towards each side. The 20 threads allows for the ladder hemstitch and narrow border to be worked across the table mat along both sides of the pattern darning.

Table mat centre tack lengthways 4 × 4 threads.

Sofia pattern

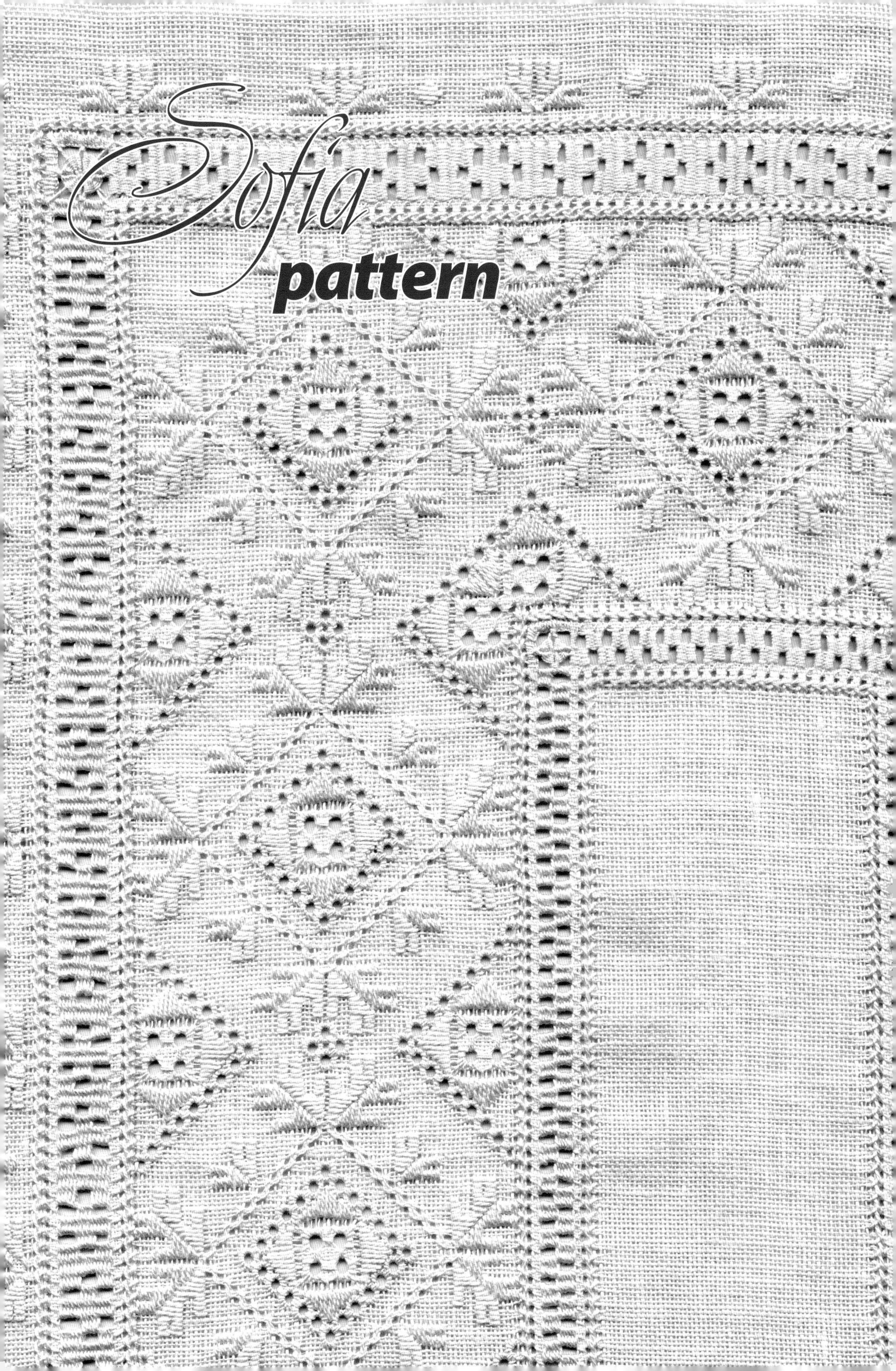

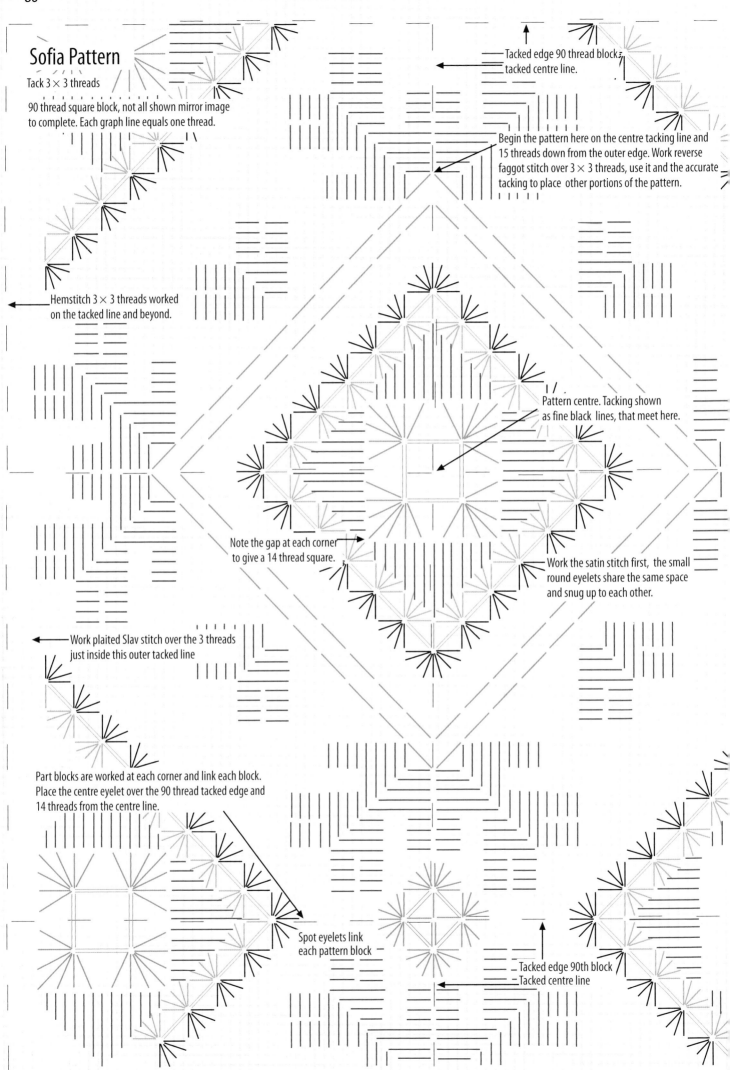

Sofia Pattern

Tack 3 × 3 threads

90 thread square block, not all shown mirror image to complete. Each graph line equals one thread.

Tacked edge 90 thread block, tacked centre line.

Begin the pattern here on the centre tacking line and 15 threads down from the outer edge. Work reverse faggot stitch over 3 × 3 threads, use it and the accurate tacking to place other portions of the pattern.

Hemstitch 3 × 3 threads worked on the tacked line and beyond.

Pattern centre. Tacking shown as fine black lines, that meet here.

Note the gap at each corner to give a 14 thread square.

Work the satin stitch first, the small round eyelets share the same space and snug up to each other.

Work plaited Slav stitch over the 3 threads just inside this outer tacked line

Part blocks are worked at each corner and link each block. Place the centre eyelet over the 90 thread tacked edge and 14 threads from the centre line.

Spot eyelets link each pattern block

Tacked edge 90th block
Tacked centre line

Sofia PATTERN

In 1948 Sofia's husband, Stephan, was sentenced to hard labour in Siberia for refusing to convert from Ukrainian Catholic to Russian Orthodoxy. In spite of the hardships she knew she would have to face, Sofia chose to go with her husband. The journey to the Siberian penal settlement took many weeks. The transport was by train and river-barge. The cold and hunger was intense. Sofia had taken her sewing machine with her, and to make life a little easier, she spent her days making clothes for locals in exchange for food. After Stephan died, Sofia stayed on in Siberia for another three years, and returned to Ukraine in 1957. This was not a happy move. She was not welcomed back. Her old friends were too frightened to help her, and she was not able to return to their own home but had to live in a one-room flat. As harsh as it was Sofia had found life better living in Siberia. In 1984 her son Orion visited Ukraine as a tourist but was unable to visit the town his mother lived in; she had to meet him in a hotel.

The Sofia pattern with a 13.5 cm deep border is worked around each side of a tray cloth. The linen shown is 25 count antique white Lauder linen purchased many years ago. The threads are DMC perle cottons Nos. 8 and 12 shade ecru. The finished size is 64 cm × 38 cm.

You will need:

- 25 count linen 70 cm × 45 cm
- Perle cottons No. 8 (2 balls) and No. 12
- Small round frame, tapestry and crewel needles
- Sharp pointed scissors, tacking threads

The stitches and threads used are:

- Satin, plaited Slav stitch, needle weaving and small motifs are worked with No. 8 perle cotton.
- Reverse faggot, small round eyelets, spot eyelet blocks and hemstitch with No. 12 perle cotton.

Instructions

- Stitches, see pages 22–25.
- Hems, page 111, woven corner fillings, page 110.
- Read the information on linen, threads, tacking, etc., pages 17–21.
- Before proceeding read Drawn thread borders, pages 104–109, for information, photographs and instructions on how to work these borders and deal with withdrawn threads. Work the short inner borders as either option 2 or 3, page 106.

Preparation:

- Straighten the linen and secure the raw edges, see page 17.
- Tack an accurate grid over 3 × 3 threads.
- The Sofia pattern is a 90 × 90 thread square block.

Begin stitching the Sofia pattern at the middle block of a long border and work towards each corner. First work the reverse faggot diamond, use it, the colour coded graph and the tacking to place other portions of the pattern.

- Small round eyelets. Work the outer row drawn black, then the inner row drawn blue. Note that they snug up to the satin stitch.

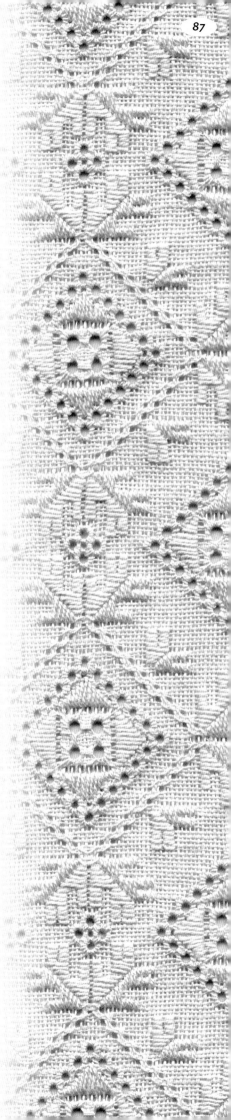

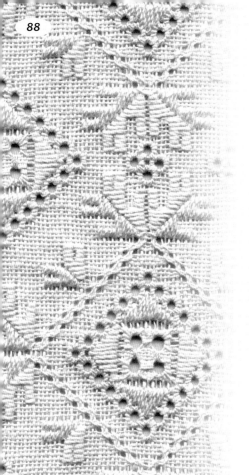

88

- Square spot eyelets drawn green are worked 3 threads inside the tacked outer edge. A small group of eyelets are placed across the 90 thread tacking.

Drawn thread needle woven inner border is No. 1, page 106, and is worked up to the tacked pattern edge. It is completed and the withdrawn threads darned back into the linen weave before the pattern can be worked at the corners. Begin at the centre of a long side. The stitch sequence is:

- Leave three threads and work plain hemstitch over the 3 × 3 threads.
- Cut 6 threads, they are not withdrawn until edged with hemstitch.
- Leave three threads and work a second line of plain hemstitch.
- It is important to have the hemstitches gathering the same threads into bundles of three.

Corner part blocks, see the photograph on page 85. Tack a diagonal line 3 × 3 threads where they meet at the inner corners. It helps to work with two needles and threads. Work the satin stitch first, but leave the centre portion on the bias until all the other parts are completed. Begin the small round eyelets on the 90 thread tacking line and 14 threads from the tacked centre. Note that there is a 'fudge point' where they meet, one eyelet is over four threads not three. The square eyelets overlap by four threads at the inner corner. Use a crewel needle to work the satin stitch on the bias, start at the centre and take one stitch into every half space at the edge of the small round eyelets.

The outer drawn thread border is No. 5, page 108, and is worked up to the tacked pattern edge. From the centre of a side the sequence for the outer border is:

- Work plain hemstitch over the 3 × 3 threads next to the tacked pattern edge.
- Cut ten threads, they are not withdrawn until edged with hemstitch.
- Work a second row of plain hemstitch over 3 × 3 threads.
- It is important to have the hemstitches gathering the same threads.

Woven Corner fillings are worked with No. 12 perle cotton left from the hemstitch. Those for the inner border will not need the diagonal stitch.

Plaited Slav stitch is worked over 3 threads just inside the 90 thread block and edges both sides of the needle woven borders.

Small motifs edge the needle weaving, use the tacking to place them. See No. 8, page 102.

Work your name and date on the reverse side of the hem.

Hem. Count the threads from the edge of the border out to hem, tack to mark fold lines. Mitre the corners and work hemstitch over 3 × 3 threads with either No. 12 perle cotton or threads withdrawn from the linen.

Congratulations! You have completed a beautiful piece of heritage embroidery that will become a treasured family heirloom.

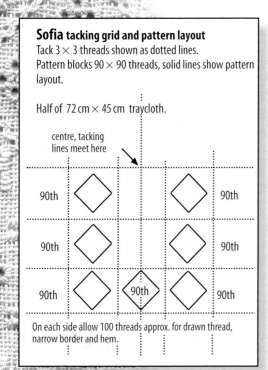

Sofia tacking grid and pattern layout
Tack 3 × 3 threads shown as dotted lines.
Pattern blocks 90 × 90 threads, solid lines show pattern layout.

Half of 72 cm × 45 cm traycloth.

centre, tacking lines meet here

90th   90th
90th   90th
90th   90th   90th

On each side allow 100 threads approx. for drawn thread, narrow border and hem.

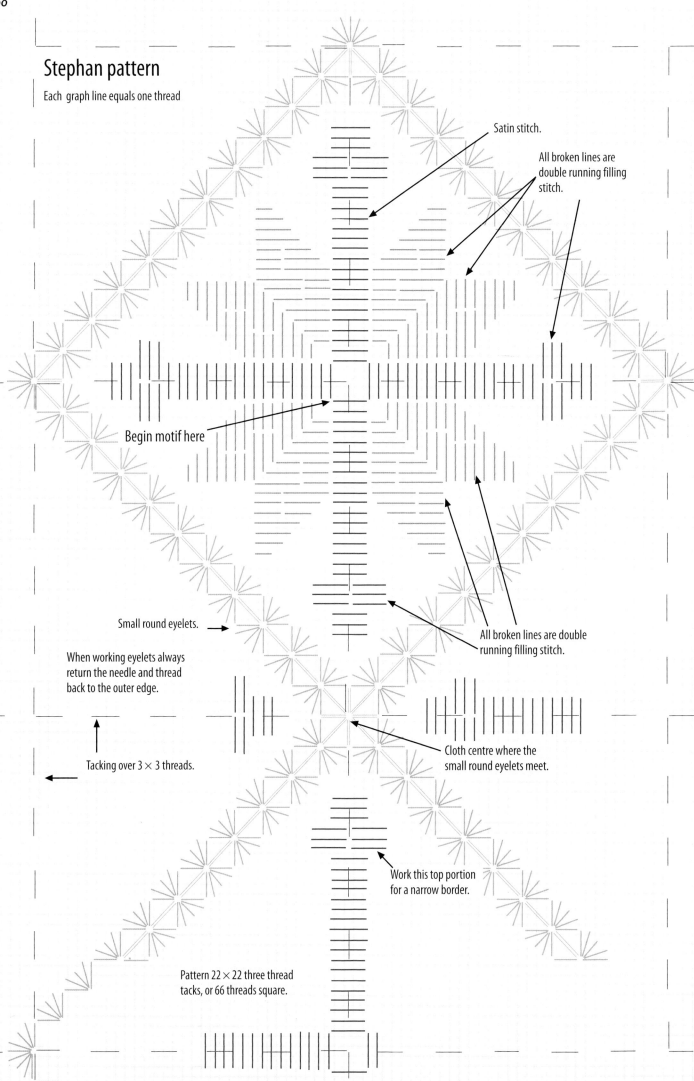

Stephan pattern

Each graph line equals one thread

Satin stitch.

All broken lines are double running filling stitch.

Begin motif here

All broken lines are double running filling stitch.

Small round eyelets.

When working eyelets always return the needle and thread back to the outer edge.

Tacking over 3 × 3 threads.

Cloth centre where the small round eyelets meet.

Work this top portion for a narrow border.

Pattern 22 × 22 three thread tacks, or 66 threads square.

Stephan PATTERN

Stephan was a Ukrainian Catholic priest of the Eastern Byzantine rite. He was married to Sofia, they had two children and lived in a township just west of the Polish–Soviet border. In 1945 Polish and Soviet Governments forcibly resettled 170 000 Ukrainians who lived in this area to Soviet Ukraine. Poles living east of that border were resettled west to their homeland. Many of those who protested against this order were shot and their houses burnt. Stephan and his Polish friend arranged to exchange houses and moved their possessions by goods-train. Back in Ukraine, Stephan found work as a cleaner and a guide at the local museum. In 1948 the Soviet Union persecuted the Ukrainian Catholic Church by demanding that all priests convert to Russian Orthodox. Stephan refused and was sent to Siberia along with many other priests and colleagues. His wife Sofia chose to go with him. Once in Siberia he was sent to work in the forests, felling trees and transporting the logs along the waterways. In 1954 he collapsed and died of a heart attack. Stephan kept a diary during those turbulent years which was published in Australia by his son.

The Stephan pattern is shown as a small runner or tray cloth with the pattern down the centre. It is finished with a drawn thread needle wrapped border with small motifs worked on the inside edge. The linen shown is Lauder 25 thread count old white, purchased many years ago. The threads are D.M.C. perle cottons Nos. 8 and 12 shade 415 grey. The finished size is 53 cm × 30 cm.

You will need:

- 25 count linen, 60 cm × 36 cm
- Perle cottons No. 8 and No. 12
- Small round frame, tapestry and crewel needles
- Small sharp pointed scissors, tacking threads

The stitches and threads are:

- Satin stitch, double running filling and small motifs are worked with No 8 perle cotton.
- Small round eyelets and drawn thread needle wrapped border and woven corner fillings are worked with No. 12 perle cotton.
- Hemstitch is worked with threads withdrawn from the linen.

Instructions:

- Read the useful information on linen threads, tacking, etc., pages 17–21.
- Drawn thread borders see pages 104–107 for information, instructions, patterns and photographs on how to work them and deal with withdrawn threads.
- Stitches, pages 22–25.
- Hems, page 111.
- Woven corner fillings, page 110.

Preparation:

- Straighten the linen and secure the raw edges.
- Tack a grid over 3 × 3 threads. It ensures accuracy and is a simple method for pattern placement.
- The Stephan pattern is 66 threads deep × 66 threads wide.

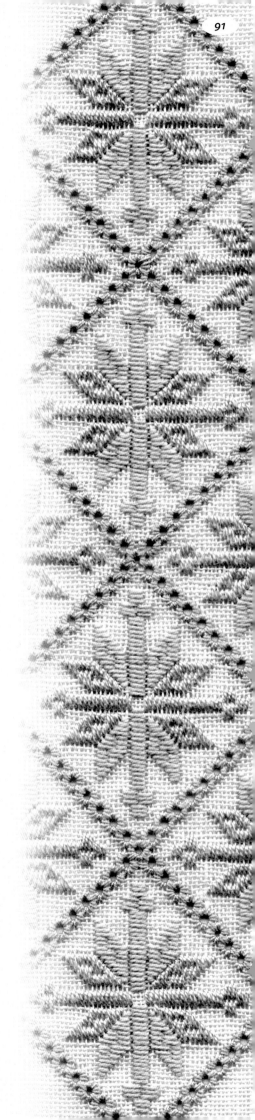

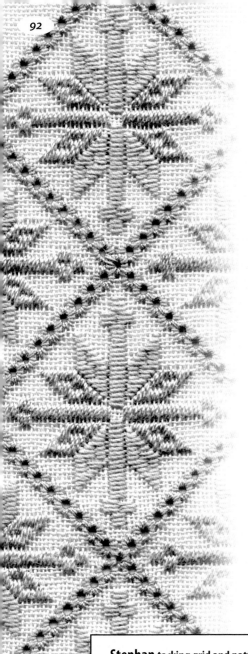

- Tack further lines each 33 threads out from the centre tacking line, then others each 33 threads apart. See the tacking grid and pattern layout,

To work the Stephan pattern use the colour coded graph. It includes the tacking shown as fine black lines. Begin the pattern at the centre of a motif and 33 threads from the centre of the mat. Work the satin stitch cross over four threads with three double running filling stitches at the end of each arm. Work the florets, note they also include double running filling stitch. See pattern graph.

Double running filling stitch seen on a 17th century towel in the Zagorsk Museum Catalogue. *Mary Thomas Dictionary of Stitches* lists it as darning-double also similar to double running, except it is a filling not an outline stitch, also known as pessante. Work it the same as double running stitch, the solid lines are the thread, the arrows show where they enter the linen, the dotted line is the thread on the underside. This stitch is the same both sides and gives a very neat appearance to the work. It is an excellent method of breaking up satin stitch worked over a wide count and gives added interest to the motif.

Small round eyelets, follow the colour coded graph. Work the outer border first drawn blue, then the inner border drawn orange. Note how they continue from one diamond shape onto the next.

Drawn thread border is worked up to the hemstitch line. The working instructions, stitches and patterns are on pages 104–109.

The stitch sequence is:

- Leave 2 threads, cut 2, leave 2 and work ladder hemstitch across these six threads.
- Cut 10 threads for the needle wrapped border No. 12, page 109. They are not withdrawn until bordered by the ladder hemstitch.
- Leave 2 threads, cut 2, leave 2 and work ladder hemstitch across them.
- Once the withdrawn threads are hanging loose at the corners, darn every second one back to the edge of the cloth.

Woven corner fillings. Lay two threads across the space both ways and weave each pair together to form a cross. Carry 2–3 threads around the cross and buttonhole over them to create the circle. See page 110.

Narrow Border. Work the top portion of the cross around the drawn thread border to complete the piece, see No. 1, page 102.

Hem. Count the threads from edge of the embroidery out to hem edge. Tack to mark the lines required. Mitre the corners and work hemstitch over 2 × 2 threads and into the ladder hemstitch that borders the drawn thread.

Work your name and date on the reverse side of the hem in a simple back stitch.

Congratulations! You have completed a beautiful piece of Ukrainian Whitework that will be enjoyed for many years.

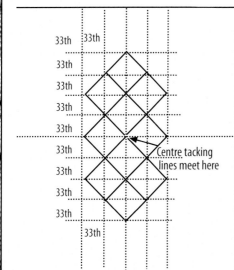

Stephan tacking grid and pattern layout
Tack 3 × 3 threads, each line both length & width is 33 threads from the next.
Dotted line is the tacking, solid lines the pattern.

33th 33th
33th
33th
33th
33th
33th Centre tacking lines meet here
33th
33th
33th
33th

Further ways to enjoy Ukrainian whitework

There are a number of ways to use the Ukrainian Whitework patterns other than those already illustrated. The small projects on the following pages offer a few suggestions to use these lovely patterns. They are also a great way to use the small scraps of linen and thread that accumulate. When adapting patterns, the tacking described on pages 20–21 is a worthwhile and accurate method to place the various motifs and borders. Use it to suit your purpose and take the guesswork out of pattern placement.

Tablecloths: When planning, it is advantageous to set the table and note where the embroidery will be seen. Instead of working a border around the hem edge, work it where it can be seen. It could be either as two or three bands of pattern across the centre width, or down the centre length. For a wider border either extend the drawn thread borders with extra rows of hem-stitch as illustrated on pages 108-109 or work a pattern in two adjoining rows. Another option is to work the main motif in a half drop layout as the Eugenie and Stephan patterns.

Runners or table scarves: many of the patterns are suitable to be worked down the centre of a narrow piece of linen as the Orion pattern. A table scarf will dress up a plain easy care, linen look cloth and keep the embroidery out of the way of the gravy and red wine.

The small projects: If these techniques are new to you, small projects are a useful starting point. Some of them would be ideal projects for grandmothers to teach young teenagers to begin learning the joys of needlework. Any of these pieces would make very acceptable gifts.

Needle books: Use one of the larger patterns for the front of a needle book, e.g., Anna, Eugenie, Maria, Olena, Orion, Sofia or Stephan. Select a small portion of the pattern for the back cover. To include pockets in the lining, make a pattern with a piece of tissue paper. Fold the tissue as required for pocket depth, this will give the measurement for the extra length of cotton fabric required. The folded lining pockets are held in place once the flannel or felt pages are stitched through all the layers. For extra pockets, the folded lining is stitched to buckram down through the centre of each side of the cover portion, see pages 96–97.

Pin cushions: Use any of the patterns to make a pin cushion to match the needle book or just to have as a useful piece.

Preparation: Whatever the project it is always worth the time and effort to secure the cut edges of linen as described on page 17. To tack a grid for pattern placement and correct thread count, see pages 20–21.

If the piece of linen is too small to hold in a frame, it can be made large enough by stitching a piece of calico or similar along the sides. Another option is to place it in the centre of a larger piece of calico, stitch around the outer edge of the linen, then cut the calico away from the back to allow the stitching to proceed.

Name and date even the smallest project. If making a gift it could also include other information stitched in simple lettering.

Band samplers are treasured needleworks from previous generations that shed a light on the skills and attitudes of past centuries. Ukrainian Whitework is a stunning technique to use for twenty-first century band samplers. There are many patterns and techniques in this book that could be included on these highly decorative needleworks that could become special family pieces.

Band samplers are usually worked on a long narrow piece of linen, with quality, fast colour thread. For the best results select patterns of various widths, include the drawn thread, needle woven and wrapped borders plus the narrow borders. Use portions of a pattern; the layout of many of them may be altered to give a border that is not as deep as illustrated. To achieve this the Stephan pattern could be worked in a similar way to the Andrij pattern with half blocks instead of full blocks. The Iryna pattern could be shortened by working fewer of the satin stitch and large round eyelet portions and just half of both the Anna and Hala patterns could be worked. This would apply to most of the other material in this book.

Another option would be to include a band of text to record family history, special events, poetry or quotations. The choices are many. If using bands of text see my earlier book *Wessex Stitchery* published in 2000. It gives details of using text in this way and includes three samplers with lettering worked as bands of pattern interspersed with bands of Wessex Stitchery patterns.

The band sampler shown on the cover and opposite is worked on 28 count Cashel linen, colour 322 sand. The threads are D.M.C. perle cottons No. 8, No. 12 and stranded cottons all shade 437.

The patterns are Mychajlo, bands of ladder and looped hemstitches, Anna, drawn thread border No. 3 edged with ladder hemstitch. The Andrij pattern, bands of ladder and looped hemstitches. Hala pattern and drawn thread border No. 7. Further bands of ladder and looped hemstitches and the Orion pattern. Not shown are drawn thread border No 6 edged with ladder hemstitch.

You will need:

- Linen: either 25, 28 or 30 count, 24 cm wide × 50 cm long, or longer
- Threads: perle No. 8, No.12, stranded, cotton-a-broder, sewing cotton

Preparation:

- Read the chapter on linen threads, tacking and other useful information, pages 17–21.
- Straighten the linen and secure the raw edges, see page 17.
- Tack a line 4 × 4 threads down the centre of the linen.
- Tack margins 8 cm out from the centre line on each side.
- Before proceeding read Drawn thread borders, pages 104–107, for information and illustrations showing how to work a single sided border and deal with withdrawn threads. To avoid the ugly gap at the end of a drawn thread border, the photograph opposite illustrates how they are linked to the edge of the linen. See "For single sided borders as table mats", page 107.

To work a band sampler:

- Begin stitching 5 cm down from the top edge, to allow for framing.

This diagram shows how the lining is folded to create the pockets for the front and back cover of this needlebook.

Small needle book. The embroidery on the cover of this small needle book is the centre portion of the Olena pattern; a smaller portion of the pattern is worked on the back cover. The fine liberty cotton lawn, lining is folded to give two pockets, one at the front and another at the back.

You will need:

- Linen, 21 cm × 14 cm, fine cotton lining, 30 cm × 22 cm
- Flannel or felt 1 piece 20 cm × 13 cm. If too white, dye it in tea
- Threads, perle No. 8, stranded and sewing cotton, tapestry and crewel needles
- The linen is Semco 30 count shade pink, threads Anchor perle No. 8 and stranded each shade 894.

The stitches and threads used are:

- Satin and buttonhole stitch, use No. 8 perle cotton.
- Square eyelets and double running stitch, two strands of stranded cotton.

Instructions:

- Read the useful information on linen, threads, tacking, etc., pages 17–21.
- Stitches are on pages 22–25, finger cord, page 26, and bobbles, page 23.

Preparation:

- Straighten the linen, then secure the raw edges with a narrow serpentine stitch to cover just the 4–5 threads at the cut edge, see page 17.
- Tack to mark the hem turn under, centre back and the centre of the cover both length and width. The width of each side of the cover is measured inside the hem allowance and the centre back tacking.
- Fold the lining up to give a pocket approximately 7–8 cm deep, leave a 1 cm seam allowance, press to hold.

To work:

- Embroider the front and back of the needle book cover.
- Tack to hold the cover, hem turn under, in place.
- Lining: fold under the hem allowance, trim and tack it to the cover.
- Join the lining to the cover with buttonhole stitch, worked between every second thread and over three threads. Include a buttonhole loop at the top of the spine to hold a thread cutter, see page 23.

Flannel pages: withdraw two threads each side of the page, to size required. Buttonhole stitch around the flannel and only cut the extra fabric away after the edge has been stitched. This keeps the flannel edge from frilling.

- Attach the page to the cover with double running stitch worked over every three linen threads and about two of the flannel. This stitching can be kept straight by checking as each stitch is made that they are always between the same two threads.
- To attach a thread cutter to the buttonhole loop at the top of the spine: Make a finger cord and thread it through the loop on the cutter. Next thread the cord through the stitched loop, at the spine. Make a bobble to attach to the cord ends, to keep the thread cutter secured to the needlebook.

The inside cover with the lining folded to make a pocket on both the front and back covers.

Needlebook with ten pockets. The cover is embroidered with a mirror image of the Orion pattern, a smaller portion is worked on the back cover. The lining is folded to give ten pockets, four at the front and four at the back and two narrow ones at the spine, between the flannel pages. The pockets are able to hold packets of needles and the stranded cotton floss holders, the narrow pockets could hold a pencil, stiletto or hedebo ring stick or other narrow tool.

You will need:

- Linen 26 cm × 16 cm, fine cotton lining, 50 cm × 28 cm
- Flannel or felt 2 pieces 24 cm × 16 cm, buckram 30 cm × 20 cm
- Perle No. 8, stranded and sewing cotton, tapestry and crewel needles
- The linen is Semco 30 count shade tea, threads Anchor perle No. 8 and stranded each shade 372. The lining is liberty cotton lawn. The cover is strengthened and pockets stitched to buckram, a fine canvas interfacing.

The stitches and threads used are:

- Satin stitch and buttonhole with No. 8 perle cotton.
- Reverse faggot, square eyelets, use two strands; chain and top stitch with three strands of stranded cotton.

Instructions:

- Read the useful information on linen, threads, tacking, etc., pages 17–21.
- Stitches are on pages 22–25, finger cord, page 26, and bobbles, page 23.

Preparation:

- Straighten the linen. Secure the raw edges 4–5 threads at the cut edge.
- Tack the hem turn under, centre back and centres each side of the cover.
- Use a square to cut the buckram to the finished size of the needle book.
- As a stitching guide, rule pencil lines on the buckram to mark the centre back and the centre of both the front and back covers.
- Lining: fold it to give two pockets, each approximately 7–8 cm deep; it needs to cover the buckram, plus a 1 cm seam allowance. The lower pocket fold should be not quite at the base of the buckram.

To work:

- Embroider the covers both front and back, then tack the hem turn under.
- Attach the folded lining to the buckram with chain stitch worked down the centre of each side of the cover. Follow the drawn pencil lines, they will be on the underside; this creates the eight pockets.
- To allow the book to fold, cut a 1 cm wide strip of buckram off at the spine.
- Lining: fold the hem allowance under and trim. Ladder stitch the lining to the cover with sewing cotton; use small stitches.
- Top stitch around the needle book, approximately 4 threads down from the edge and over 3 × 3 threads to hold the cover, lining and buckram together.
- Flannel pages: see page 96. Attach the pages to the cover with double running stitch, catch in the buckram. Leave a 1.5 cm strip at the spine or width required between the pages for the two narrow pockets.
- To attach a thread cutter see pages 23 and 96.

This diagram shows how the lining is folded to create the ten pockets for front and back covers of the lining.

The inside cover shows the four pockets and the chain stitch at the centre and through the buckram that divides them. Four further pockets are on the back cover and two narrow ones between the flannel pages.

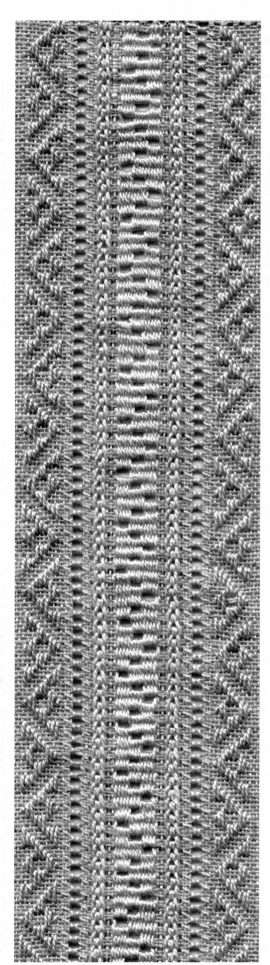

Table mats. *As well as the tables mats worked with the merezhka and pattern darning techniques, Ukrainian whitework offers other options. The drawn thread table mats illustrated use needle woven borders that have been enlarged by including both the ladder and looped hemstitch. Each mat is finished with a narrow border worked to edge the drawn thread work. Two of the enlarged borders can be seen on page 108. Also on page 108, border No. 9 illustrates another option for table mats that could be applied to any of the drawn thread borders given. The information given with the band sampler, includes how to narrow patterns; any of these would be ideal for this purpose. Table mats each worked with a different pattern add interest to a table setting and would make wonderful wedding gifts.*

You will need:

- Linen: half a metre will be enough for four table mats, this allows a little extra for threads to use for hemstitching, see Threads on page 18
- Threads: perle cotton No. 8 and No. 12
- The mats are worked on Semco linen, natural with Anchor perle cottons Nos. 8 and 12 shade 388. The finished size of each is 45 cm × 30 cm.

The stitches and threads used are:

- Needle weaving, looped hemstitch and narrow borders with No 8 perle cotton.
- Ladder hemstitch with No. 12 perle cotton.

Instructions:

- Read the useful information on linen, threads, tacking, etc., pages 17–21.
- Drawn thread needle woven and wrapped borders are on pages 104–107.
- Use the tacking diagram and preparation instructions for the merezhka table mats, pages 61–62.

Preparation:

- Straighten the linen and secure the cut edge with machine stitching.
- Tack the three lines required for hems, plus 14 cm down the centre of the table mat.
- Cut the threads required at the centre of the border and only withdraw the threads that hemstitch will be worked over, see page 108, borders 4 and 8.

To work the table mats:

The hemstitches are worked from right to left across the border. Begin the ladder hemstitch 15 threads down from the tacked hemstitch line. It is worked across the border and gathers the threads together into bundles of three. Follow with the looped hemstitch making sure that each hemstitch gathers the same bundles of three threads. Repeat for the two lower rows of hemstitch.

The needle weaving and narrow borders are begun at the centre of the border to allow them to finish at the same place each side of the mat. Withdraw these threads back 6–8 cm at a time. Do not cut withdrawn threads off, pages 105–106 illustrate how to deal with them.

Read "For single sided borders as table mats", page 107, for information on how to avoid the ugly gap between the linen and needle woven border.

Lavender bags. Small decorative lavender bags filled with the dried fragrant flowers make lovely gifts for special people. The pattern on the green lavender bag is a portion of the Mychajlo pattern. It is lined with a patterned liberty lawn fabric and includes a channel for the finger cord that is stitched through both fabrics. The blue lavender bag features the Olya pattern worked one below the other. This bag is unlined and large round eyelets have been worked to carry the finger cord. Both lavender bags have been joined with the antwerp edging stitch and have draw-string finger cords finished with bobbles to close the bag.

You will need:

- Linen: 11–12 cm × 46 cm, or it could be in two pieces
- Lining: 12 cm × 46 cm, perle cotton No. 8 and stranded cotton

The stitches and threads used are:

- Satin stitch, finger cord and bobbles with No. 8 perle cotton.
- The single and reverse faggot stitches plus large round eyelets and antwerp edging stitch are all worked with two strands of stranded cotton.

Instructions:

- Read the useful information on linen, threads, tacking, etc., pages 17–21.
- Stitches are on pages 22–25, finger cords page 26, bobbles page 23.

Preparation:

- Straighten the linen. Secure the raw edges with a narrow machine serpentine stitch to cover just the 4 threads at the cut edge, see page 17.
- Tack to mark the hem turn under, 4–5 threads from the cut edge, the draw thread channel 4 cm down from the top edge and the centre front and back.
- Lining: cut to size and press the hem allowance under.

Work: The pattern of your choice.

For a lined bag: The linen is Semco Willow grey, thread Anchor perle 8 and stranded cotton shade 858. The pattern Mychajlo page 64.

- Tack the lining to the linen. For the draw thread channel work two rows of double running stitch through both fabrics, each 1 cm apart. Buttonhole around the open ends of the channel.

For an unlined bag: The linen is Semco Grey blue, thread Anchor perle 8 and stranded cotton shade 850. The pattern Olya, page 72.

- Stitch a straight line of large round eyelets on the draw thread channel tacking, they are each four threads apart, see page 24.

For both bags:

- Work antwerp buttonhole stitch around the four sides of the bag, between every second thread and over 3–4 threads.
- A second round of antwerp buttonhole is stitched into the edge of the first, below the drawstring channel to join the linen to form a bag,
- Make finger cords and attach bobbles to them.

$\mathcal{B}ook\ marks.$ Portions of many of the patterns in this book could be used for book marks. They use small scraps of linen and thread and are a useful way to practise some of the patterns and methods of working. Merezhka Poltavska and the needle woven and wrapped borders make excellent bookmarks. They and the pattern darning borders would not need to be neatened with a lining. Those with a variety of stitches would.

You will need:

- Linen: approximately 8 cm × 30 cm, fine cotton lining 8 cm × 22 cm.
- Bond-a-web or Vliesofix, perle cottons No. 8, No. 12 and stranded cotton.

Instructions:

- Read the useful information on linen, threads, tacking, etc., pages 17–21.
- An unlined bookmark with a buttonhole edge should be secured with machine stitching, see page 17.

Preparation:

- Straighten the linen and cut to size required, include a fringe.
- Tack down the centre of the bookmark.
- Lining: cut straight and a little larger than required.

The stitches and threads used are:

- Follow the instructions for the pattern of your choice and work it down the centre.

For all book marks: Withdraw two threads of the linen on each side of the embroidered area to the size required. The fringe is beyond this. See "To neaten and secure cut edges" of small projects, page 17.

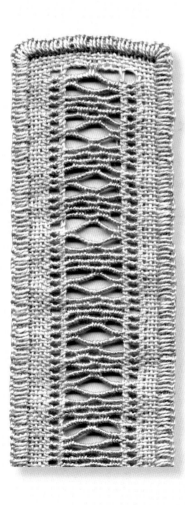

For a lined book mark: the linen is Semco Salmon, threads Anchor perle 8 and stranded cotton shade 336.

- Bond the lining to the reverse side of the linen with bond-a-web or similar.
- Work buttonhole stitch around the four sides with two strands of stranded cotton, through both fabrics, between each thread and over 4 threads.
- Once completed, carefully cut the fabrics away from the buttonhole edge on the two long sides. If a fringe is included, pull the lining away from the linen and cut it off. Withdraw the threads for the fringe.

For an unlined bookmark: The linen is grey green purchased years ago, the threads D.M.C. perle Nos. 8 and 12 shade 927.

Work either buttonhole stitch over 4 threads and between each thread or two rows of plain hemstitch over 3 × 3 threads. It is worked around the four sides and up to the withdrawn threads around the embroidered portion.

- Once completed, carefully cut the linen away from the neatened edge on the long sides.

Fringe: Linen threads could be withdrawn for a fringe at both ends, or just one, or not included.

Fringe not shown on those illustrated.

Merezhka Zatiahanka is a little known drawn thread technique worked with linen and thread that are an exact match to achieve the result required. The stitching begins at the bottom of the piece and works up to the top. For further design ideas that could be worked on table runners or mats look at fairisle knitting patterns.

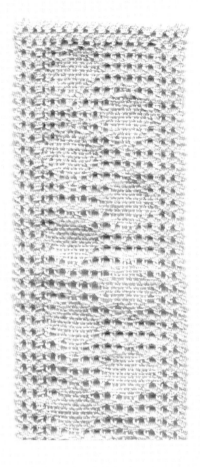

You will need:

Linen and thread the exact match. The example shown is a bookmark worked on 25 count cream Dublin linen with DMC No. 12 perle cotton, shade ecru.

Stitches:

Plain hemstitch, see page 17, and darning.

Instructions:

Read the useful information on linen, threads, tacking, etc., pages 17–21.

Each row of stitching is three threads deep. The thread count for cutting is: cut and withdraw one thread just above the last row of stitching and darn it out to the edge of linen. Leave two threads.

Tacking is drawn as fine black lines. The black dotted lines, some with an arrow, show the needle and thread carried on the underside to be in place to work the next group of stitches. A straight stitch is made prior to darning, see the graph.

To work:

Follow the graph. The first line of stitching is plain hemstitch worked over 3 × 3 threads to border the pattern. Once completed cut, withdraw and darn the next thread out the edge of the linen.

To begin the pattern work plain hemstitch over 3 × 2 threads for the number of stitches shown on the graph for each section of the pattern.

Darning fills the space left by the withdrawn thread and is worked in the same sequence as the woven thread; this will hold the darning line in place. It takes the needle and thread to the next group of plain hemstitch. Continue the pattern for the length required.

To finish the bookmark darn both the withdrawn and perle threads into the weave to become part of the fringe. Withdraw two threads to size required. Work two rows of hemstitch over 3 × 3 threads around the four sides gathering in and securing the darned threads. The hemstitch should be worked firmly at the edge to avoid the linen fraying.

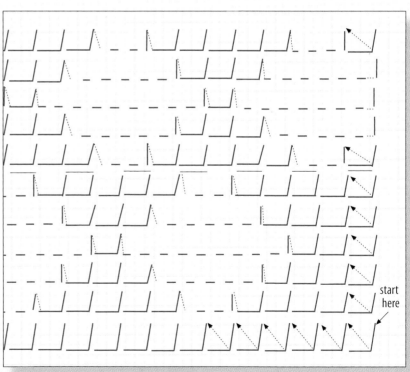

start here

Only after the edge is completed, cut the extra linen off up to the hemstitch edge. This ensures that the edge does not frill. Withdraw threads for a fringe as required.

See "To neaten and secure cut edges" of small projects, page 17.

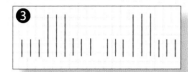

Narrow Borders

Each graph line equals one thread

Narrow borders of small motifs worked at the outer edges of a pattern are one of the features of Ukrainian Whitework that make this technique different from similar styles of needlework.

Some of the narrow borders are portions of the pattern, others link to it by the similarity of shape to the main pattern. For a large project, e.g., Maria tablecloth and Sofia tray cloth, the narrow border motifs are placed across the centre tacking and at the edge of each pattern block. Other motifs will be worked closer to each other as a border, e.g., Anna pattern and the pattern darning and merezhka table mats. For smaller projects the narrow border could be worked at the outer edge only. The inside edge is usually bordered with ladder hemstitch.

Use the tacking to place the motifs. Most of the borders shown are worked in satin stitch with No. 8 perle cotton. Eyelets are worked with No. 12 perle cotton or equivalent.

The narrow borders, or small motifs can be enlarged or reduced in size by changing the thread count and the spacing between each block or working three threads instead of the two shown or over two instead of three. Borders 5 and 9 have been altered this way, see the Anna pattern and pattern darning table mats. Border 4, Orion pattern has been enlarged to 11 for the Maria table cloth. The adjoining blocks of satin stitch, of borders 1 and 9 have been worked for some projects as double running filling stitch, see page 22 for working instructions.

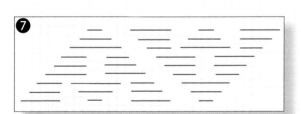

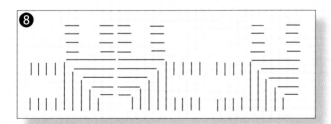

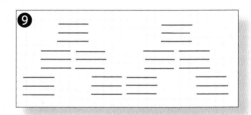

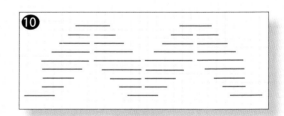

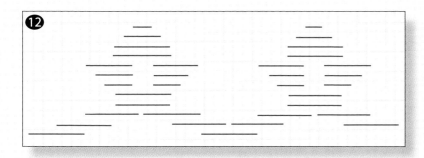

Verkhoploot narrow borders feature on work from Poltava and where counted satin stitch is popular. It can be worked as a single row, or as shown to create triangles. It is worked with No. 8 perle cotton in the same colours as the main borders. It is also known as topwinder and would seem to be unique to Ukraine. Verkhoploot is a useful border to work beside drawn thread borders. It features on the Andrij, Daria and Hala patterns. The straight vertical base stitches are drawn red. The rows that wind around the straight stitches are drawn orange.

Diagram 1 shows that the base line of stitching is worked from right to left. For a long border, row one would be worked the full length. The black dotted lines indicate where the thread travels on the underside.

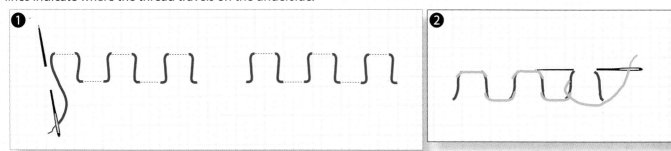

Diagram 2 illustrates the first row of top winding. It is worked from left to right. The needle is taken under the straight vertical stitch for the threads to be in place to lay across the top and the base of the vertical stitches. The needle is only taken to the back of the work where shown.

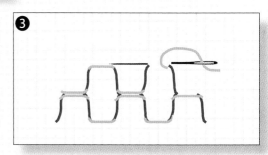

Diagram 3 shows that a second row of vertical stitches has been worked from right to left and the thread top wound around them from left to right.

Diagram 4 repeats the previous rows, but this time there are only two vertical stitches and a triangle has been created.

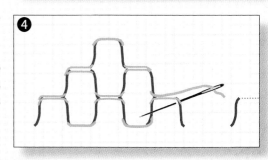

Return to diagram 1, the needle and thread are carried to the next group of straight stitches ready to work another triangle. If wanted back stitches over three threads could be worked to join each triangle as the thread is carried to the following group.

Drawn thread borders are a feature of Ukrainian Whitework. They enrich this style of work and are a factor in it being different from other traditional techniques. They are known as Merezhka, from the simplest single line of hemstitch to the wide borders and various methods of needle weaving, wrapping and layering. There is a range of working methods and some would seem to be unique to Ukraine. Drawn thread is the technique where fabric threads are cut, every second one is withdrawn, the others are darned back into the weave to be worked over. This avoids the ugly double weave when the threads were just darned back over 2–3 threads, and it is very much more secure than other methods. It also makes it possible to stitch the pattern at the corners.

Preparation: Important: please read all this information before beginning a project

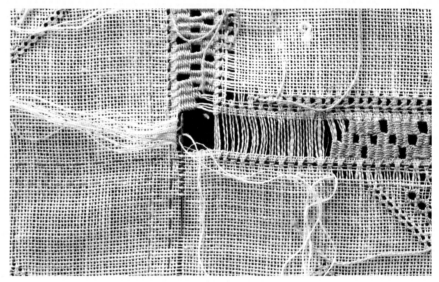

This shows that the inner band of needleweaving is worked and the withdrawn threads are darned out to the edge of the linen before the pattern can be stitched at the corners. To darn withdrawn threads out to the edge of the linen see page 106.

Hemstitches to edge drawn thread borders:

Before cutting, first edge both sides of an even number of threads with one of the hemstitches shown, page 105. This gathers them into bundles of either two, three or four ready for the needle weaving or wrapping. The corners are not stitched at this stage.

It is important to have the various hemstitches gathering the same threads across the border into bundles.

• Threads are not withdrawn until both sides of the border are hemstitched.

• For a long border begin at the centre tacking line and work towards each corner.

• For single sided borders like table mats, band samplers and antimacassars, see page 107. It gives instructions on how to avoid the ugly gap between the linen and needleweaving.

• Ladder and plain hemstitches are worked with No. 12 perle cotton or similar.

• Looped hemstitch is worked with No. 8 perle cotton.

To begin darn the perle cottons into the weave of the cloth and work over them. Finish threads off in the back of the work.

Plain hemstitch gathers the linen threads into bundles. It can be worked over 2 × 2, or 4 × 4 threads as well as the three shown. When edging needle weaving have the straight bar furthermost away from the weaving, that way it helps to keep the woven border flat.

Ladder hemstitch is two rows of single or plain hemstitch worked to face each other, with two cut and withdrawn threads between. It is worked across six threads for a 2 × 2 hemstitch, or eight threads for a 3 × 3 hemstitch.

Looped hemstitch is a single feather stitch worked in two continuous lines that face each other. It is worked across six threads with the two centre ones cut and withdrawn. The needle picks up three threads and only enters the weave to start and finish the thread. When back at the centre and working in the opposite direction, bring the thread up into the first stitch made to avoid a gap. Looped hemstitch looks similar to raised chain band and seems to be unique to Ukraine.

Before cutting any threads measure the length of fabric thread from the centre of a border back to the corner to ensure that the withdrawn threads will be long enough to darn out to the edge of the cloth.

For short borders see page 106, it gives options to choose from.

For single sided border as table mats, see page 106.

Do not cut withdrawn threads off. Decide which method to deal with them. They will be darned out to the edge of the linen. See the photographs illustrating this method.

Once the hemstitching is worked and the length of withdrawn thread known, cut the threads where selected ready for needle weaving or wrapping.

Withdraw the threads back about 6–8 cm at a time. If too long a length is withdrawn it could distort the fabric weave. Hold the work firmly in a small round frame, the withdrawn threads can either be held under the frame or pin while working.

To neaten withdrawn threads

Once the withdrawn linen threads meet those from the opposite side and are all hanging loose at the corner, darn every second one out to the edge of cloth as shown. Work with only two adjoining threads at a time, select the best of the two for darning and withdraw the other. All darning to be accurate to the weave of the linen, if not it will show.

If more than one border as the photograph shows, deal with the innermost one first. The photograph shows looped hemstitch.

Once the withdrawn threads have been darned back into the linen further stitching can be worked over that area. This method creates an inner selvedge edge and gives a superior finish to the work, there is no bulk of double threads and no possibility of them springing out.

Option 1. For long borders

The needleweaving or wrapping is worked along two adjoining borders as the photographs show. Neither the pattern or the hemstitch is worked at the corners until after the withdrawn threads have been darned out to the

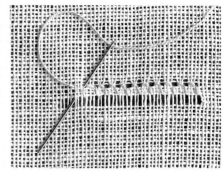

Plain hemstitch.

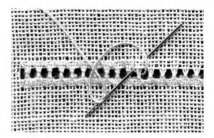

Ladder hemstitch.

Looped hemstitch.

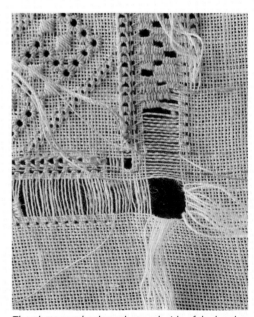

The photographs show that each side of the border is worked and that the needleweaving nearly meets at the corner before dealing with the withdrawn threads.

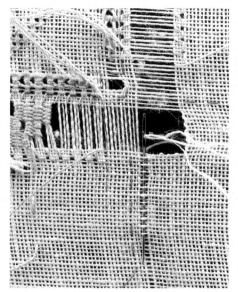

The last withdrawn thread is being darned out to the edge of the linen. An inner selvedge edge has been created.

edge of the cloth. The photograph on page 104 shows all the threads pulled back at the corner. They are not cut off. The photograph opposite illustrates the needle darning the last of the withdrawn threads into the weave of the linen. It also shows the inner selvedge edges that have been created. These new edges are not pulled tight, but sit as the weave of the cloth. On page 110 are photographs and text illustrating how this 'made' corner will be finished with a decorative woven filling.

Option 2. If threads are too short or shred and break, new threads can be withdrawn from the edge of the linen or a spare piece kept for the purpose. They need to be double the length from the inner corner to the edge of the cloth. Use a tapestry needle with the new thread and leave a tail long enough to reach the outer edge. Withdraw the first short thread. Begin at the inner corner and darn the new thread into the space left by the damaged thread. Rethread the needle with the tail, withdraw the second short or damaged thread and darn the tail into that space. Repeat until completed.

Option 3. For short inner borders as a tray cloth. Work hemstitch to edge this portion and leave the corners unstitched as the photograph illustrates. Work with adjoining pairs of thread and only one pair at a time. Withdraw a thread of the linen from the left hand edge of the cloth back to the needle woven border at the right hand side. Repeat, but this time the thread is withdrawn from the right hand edge of the cloth back to the needle woven border at the left hand side. This method gives a thread long enough to be darned out to the edge of the fabric to replace the withdrawn thread. Repeat until completed. The photograph shows the thread of the second pair being darned out to the edge of the cloth.

Option 4. For the narrow inner borders of ladder or looped hemstitch only, as in the Andrij and Hala mats. If there are only two threads to be cut and withdrawn, they can be darned into the weave to be covered with hemstitch or hidden under stitching.

Option 3 for short borders. It shows the needle darning the last thread of the second pair out to the edge of the linen.

For single sided borders as table mats and antimacassars, work the hem-stitches in the same direction, from right to left. However the needle weaving or wrapping is begun at the centre and worked out to each side; this is to allow it to finish at the same place each side of the mat. Include the new selvedge as a bundle of threads to link and anchor the needle weaving to the hem. This avoids the ugly gap between the linen and needle woven border. The new selvedge needs to be three threads within the hemstitch line, see table mats, page 98.

To finish off perle cottons at the inner selvedge corner. Darn the No. 8 perle cotton into the 'new selvedge edge'. It will be hidden under the but-tonhole stitch that will be worked over it, then carry it up through the needle-woven tubes at the corner to strengthen them and support the woven corner filling, see photograph 1, page 110.

Use any **No. 12 perle cotton** left from the hemstitching to work buttonhole stitch over the new selvedge edge and woven corner filling, see page 110.

To settle darned threads into the weave: while the linen is held taut in the frame, scratch the back of the rewoven portion and the darned threads will settle back into place and hardly show.

Needle Weaving

Choose either a needle woven or wrapped border, the thread count required for each is given with the photographs. Begin at the centre of a side and work out to each end of the border. Needle weaving is worked with No. 8 perle cotton in a tapestry needle while the linen is firmly held in a small round frame. Darn over and under and back and forth for the number of times required to cover the bundles of thread. The depth of each portion of weaving depends upon the pattern and the number of threads withdrawn. Some borders can be divided into three, others four or five. Use the needle to beat the weaving in place. The working thread can be carried up through the needle woven bundles either on the front or the back of the work to be in place to weave the various portions of the pattern. The carried thread does not show and is well hidden.

Needle woven border 1.

To bring in a new length of perle cotton either carry it under the hem-stitched edge or lay it up and down alongside the bundles of threads to be worked over. The simplest way to do this is to darn the thread into the linen; this holds it firm while stitching proceeds, the tail is cut off later.

To **finish off perle cotton** carry it under the woven tubes. For both starting and finishing thread, the length should be at least 5–7 cm.

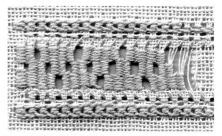

Needle woven border 2.

Border 1 shows a very simple narrow needle woven border worked across 6 threads. It can be seen on the inner border Sofia pattern. The thread count is leave 3 threads, cut 6, leave 3.

Border 2 is worked on the Maria tablecloth and includes both looped and plain hemstitch. The thread count is: leave 2 threads, cut 2, leave 5, cut 10. Leave 5, cut 2, leave 2. This border is also shown on No. 8 to illustrate how any of them can be deepened.

Border 3 is worked on the Iryna mat and illustrates how the woven bundles of thread link into each other. It is worked over 10 threads, and like border 4, could also be worked over 12. The thread count is leave 3 threads, cut 2, leave 3, cut 10, leave 3, cut 2, leave 3.

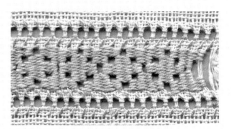

Needle woven border 3.

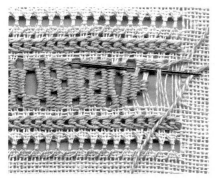

Needle woven border 4.

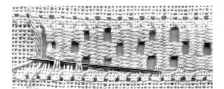

Needle woven border 5.

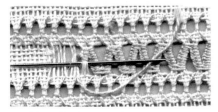

Needle woven border 6.

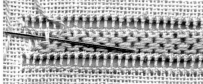

Needle woven border 7.

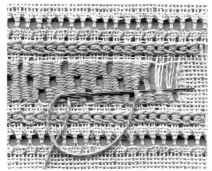

Needle woven border 8.

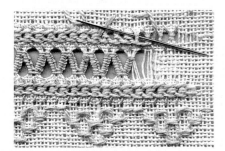

Needle woven border 9.

Border 4 features on the Olena antimacassar and is another border that could be worked over 10 threads. It illustrates the way that the bundles are linked into each other and includes both the ladder and looped hemstitches to give a wider border. The thread count is leave 2 threads, cut 2, leave 4, cut 2, leave 3, cut 12, leave 3, cut 2, leave 4, cut 2.

Border 5 is seen on the Sofia pattern and is edged with a plain hemstitch. The photograph shows the space left at the centre of the last bundle where the bundles of thread will be linked together. Weave over the two bundles; once the centre third is reached, the weaving is over four bundles, then back to two bundles to complete the group. Either count the number of rows of weaving required to cover a bundle of threads, or go by the appearance; either way is correct. The thread count is leave 3 threads, cut 2, leave 3, cut 10, leave 3, cut 2, leave 3.

Border 6 is edged with either ladder or looped hemstitch. A simple buttonhole stitch is worked over a bundles of three threads with No 12 perle cotton or similar. They are drawn into a zig zag pattern by working over two bundles of threads at the beginning of each group. This border would seem to be unique to Ukraine. The thread count is leave 2 threads, cut 2 leave 2, cut 6, leave 2, cut 2, leave 2. To work towards the opposite corner and complete a side, begin back at the centre again, anchor the thread to the first made bundle to allow the stitching to lie flat as you work towards the opposite corner.

Border 7 features on the Andrij and Olya mats and is another drawn thread method that is most possibly unique to Ukraine where it is known as "Merezhka Verkhoploot". It is worked the same as smocking, but over a drawn thread grid and like smocking it is worked in just one direction. It is edged with ladder hemstitch. The thread count is leave 2 threads, cut 2, leave 2, cut 4, leave 2, cut 2, leave 2. Three rows of stitching cover the four cut and withdrawn threads.

Border 8 shows how border No. 2 has been deepened by using both the ladder and looped hemstitches. It also illustrates how the needle weaves under and over the gathered bundles of threads to create the pattern. The thread count for this is: leave 3 threads, cut 2, leave 4, cut 2, leave 3, cut 10, leave 3, cut 2, leave 4, cut 2, leave 2. Border 8 has been worked on the place mats that illustrate further ways of enjoying Ukrainian whitework, page 93. These would make most acceptable gifts for special occasions.

Border 9 shows another way of using both the looped and ladder hemstitches to provide an interesting combination of stitch and texture. This time the looped hemstitch is worked over the bars of the ladder hemstitch. The thread count is leave 3 threads, cut 2, leave 3, cut 6, leave 3, cut 2, leave 3. The Verkhoploot border edges the band of drawn thread to give a grouping of techniques that are unique to Ukraine, see page 103.

Verkhoploot — Top winder

"Is known to have various names in different areas of Ukraine. Verkhoploot is done in two stages. First the rows of verticle stitches [are] worked. Next without catching the fabric, the needle goes under every verticle stitch from left to right, changing its point up or down."

The Art of Ukrainian Embroidery, Olena Kulynych-Stakhurska.

Border 10 is edged with two rows of ladder hemstitch. Though not used for any of the examples of Ukrainian whitework included, it illustrates another method of deeping a border. The thread count is, leave two threads, cut 2, leave 2, cut 2, leave 2, cut 10, leave 2, cut 2, leave 2, cut 2, leave 2.

Needle wrapping

This lovely technique is often seen on embroidery from around the Baltic region and is known in Ukraine as needle weaving with winding.

For wrapping use either No. 12 perle cotton or two strands of stranded cotton in a tapestry needle. The thread is wrapped around the bundles the number of times the pattern requires; then the bundles are joined together with a figure-of-eight weaving. This forms the pattern. When working the thread will be on the left hand side of the bundle and taken over the bundle of threads.

Start wrapping at the centre of a side, and wrap the middle bundle of threads from the top to the bottom, straight without any linking. From the second bundle and as the wrapping proceeds, weave the bundles together where shown to create the patterns. The linking weaving is worked over the wrapping of the previous bundle.

To work hold the linen firmly in a small round frame. Start threads the same as for needleweaving. To finish them off use a crewel needle as there are not any woven tubes to easily hide them under.

Border 11 features on the Hala mat, see pages 43–46. The thread count is leave 2 threads, cut 2, leave 2, cut 6, leave 2, cut 2, leave 2.

Border 12 has been worked on the Stephan traycloth, see page 89. The thread count is leave 2 threads, cut 2, leave 2, cut 10, leave 2, cut 2, leave 2.

The thread count can be changed if wanting a wider or narrower border or using a different fabric. Remember always an even thread count for darning the withdrawn threads into the linen. It is worthwhile to work these borders on a sampler before working them on the masterpiece. These practice samplers become valuable reference material for future projects.

All the needle woven and wrapped borders illustrated were worked on 25 count linen. The needle weaving is worked with Anchor No. 8 perle cotton shades 387 and 388. The needle wrapping with Anchor No. 12 perle cotton shade 387.

To weave a figure-of-eight the needle and thread are taken across two bundles to link them together, brought out above the linking stitch, across it and down between the two bundles and out to the left to be in place to continue wrapping. If working up a wrap the thread will be brought out below the linking stitch, taken over it, then out to the left to be in place to continue wrapping.

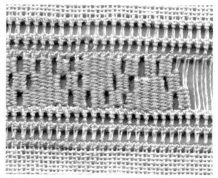

Needle woven border 10.

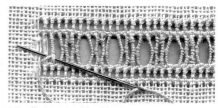

Needle wrapped border 11.

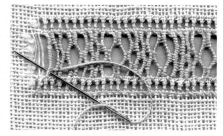

Needle wrapped border 12.

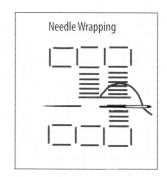

Needle Wrapping

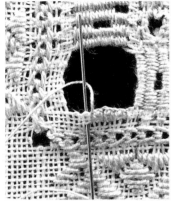

1. Buttonhole stitch worked around the new selvedge edge.

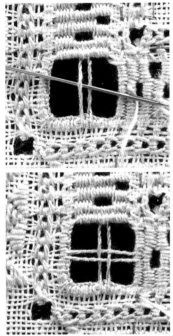

2. Both photographs show how threads are laid in a weave across the corner and twisted around each.

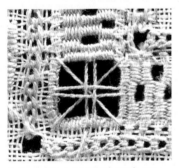

3. For a larger corner threads are laid on the diagonal.

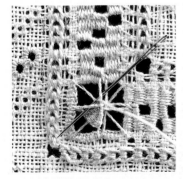

Woven corner fillings

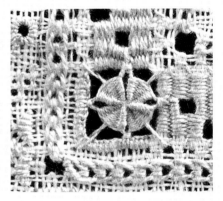

When the needle weaving is completed, the inner space created at the corners can be filled with a decorative woven filling. To work the fillings use No. 12 perle cotton and have the linen firmly held in a small round frame.

Darn the No. 8 perle threads left over from the needle weaving, into the weave of the new selvedge edge, or carry them under the buttonhole stitching once it is worked. This will strengthen the space to support the woven filling.

Work buttonhole stitch with the No. 12 perle cotton left from the hemstitching, over the three threads at the inner selvedge edge. To begin anchor the thread into the edge of the needle weaving, see photograph 1.

Lay No. 12 perle cotton across the empty corner, both horizontal and vertical to make a two thread weave at the centre. To keep the 'made' threads firm, twist them around each other on the return journey, see photograph 2.

For a ten–twelve thread corner or larger space, extra threads can be laid from corner to corner; they will also be twisted on the return journey, see photograph 3.

Weave the filling shown with No. 12 perle cotton. Start the weaving at the centre and weave across each quarter as photograph 4 shows. To carry the thread to where required twist it around the laid threads.

For a six to eight thread corner the diagonal line is not required, weave over two threads instead of the three shown, see the inner corner of the Sophia tray cloth, page 85.

Other options are: lay a double thread weave as shown in photograph 2 and either needle weave over them or wrap the made threads. Another option is to needle weave the 'made' threads, then carry perle cotton No. 12 two or three times around the crossed centre to form a circle, then work buttonhole over them (see photograph below).

To work a Spider's web filling lay the No. 12 perle cotton as shown in photograph 3 and back stitch around the laid threads.

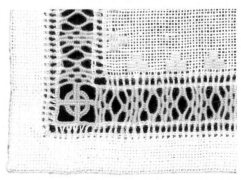

Corner filling, Stephan pattern.

4. Weave the filling across each quarter, begin at the centre and work out towards the edge.

Hems with mitred corners

To stitch a neat hem with a perfect mitred corner: the preparation is most important. First decide where the hem edge will be and the depth of hem. Most of the hems shown are over twelve threads and have either an eight or ten thread turn under. To find the hem edge use the centre tacking lines that are still in place to count the threads from the edge of the embroidery to where the edge of the hem will be. Tack accurately along this line. Each side of the cloth should have the three tacked lines that begin and finish at the edge of the linen, see diagram 1. Do not secure the tacking stitches as they need to be able to be withdrawn easily once hemstitching is completed. Keep the stitches short; it is easier to be accurate if they are under and over no more than five or six threads.

The second line to tack is the turn under. To keep the hem flat it should be two threads less than the hem. The third line to tack is the stitch line, this could be only at the corners. It is always the same depth between the hem edge and stitch line and the hem edge and turn under.

If the linen needs trimming, neaten and secure the cut edges, see page 17.

To prepare the mitre: fold the linen over at the corner on the hemstitch line and position the corner tacking to be on top of the tacked lines. Pin to hold in place as diagram 2 shows. Repeat for the adjoining corner. Fold over the hem edge and press along the tacked line with your fingers, not an iron. Fold the turn under tacked line and finger press to hold it firm. Place it on top of the stitch line and pin to hold. Join the mitred corner, use a fine needle and the thread for the hemstitching. Darn the thread into the folded corner and hold in place with two back stitches. Begin at the top corner and work ladder stitch between the two folded edges as diagram 3 shows. Pull the edges together every three or four stitches. It is possible once the first ladder stitches have been worked to fold the corner to have the edges uppermost. This way the needle enters the fold easily. Once the mitre has been joined with ladder stitch, lift the corner and cut the extra linen off just above the hemstitch line. See ladder stitch diagram, page 23.

To stitch hems: Pin the hem in place, check that it is lying on the straight of the grain of the linen; the pattern tacking threads are useful for this. Use the thread left from the mitred corner and work antique hemstitches over the number of threads that the pattern requires. For Ukrainian Whitework it is generally over three threads, though some patterns are over two and only a few over four threads. See Antique hemstitch, page 23.

Hemstitch with threads withdrawn from the linen: If unable to get a matching No. 12 perle or similar, or not wanting the hem to be too obvious, use threads withdrawn from the weave of the linen. For some linens they need to be twisted as the antique hemstitch proceeds. See threads, page 18.

Picot hem edge: as the Eugenie mat. Work ladder hemstitch across the eight threads up to the hem edge with No. 12 perle cotton or similar. Fold the ladder hemstitch through the centre. Fold the turn under hem line, pin to hold and stitch the hem in place with antique hemstitch. See page 105 for ladder stitch instructions.

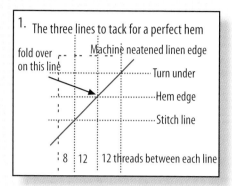

1. The three lines to tack for a perfect hem

fold over on this line — Machine neatened linen edge — Turn under — Hem edge — Stitch line

8 | 12 | 12 threads between each line

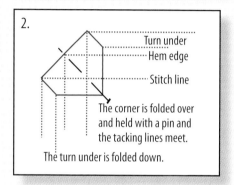

2.

Turn under
Hem edge
Stitch line

The corner is folded over and held with a pin and the tacking lines meet.
The turn under is folded down.

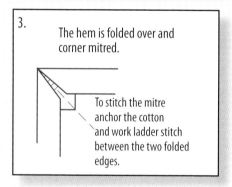

3. The hem is folded over and corner mitred.

To stitch the mitre anchor the cotton and work ladder stitch between the two folded edges.

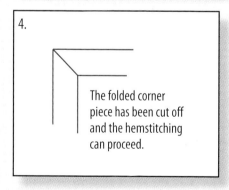

4.

The folded corner piece has been cut off and the hemstitching can proceed.

Bibliography and further reading

History

Conquest, Robert. (1986). *The Harvest of Sorrow. Soviet Collectivization and the Terror-Famine.* New York: Oxford University Press.

Dalton, Meredith. (2002). *Culture Shock Ukraine.* Oregon: Times Editions Pte Ltd.

Early Russian Embroidery in the Zagorsk Museum Collection. (1983). *Catalogue of Ecclesiastical and Ornamental from the 15th–17th century.* Russia.

Graham-Campbell, James and Kidd, Dafydd. (1980). *The Vikings.* London: British Museum.

Larousse Encyclopedia of Byzantine and Medieval Art. (1981). London: Hamlyn.

Kardash, Peter. (1991). *Ukraine its History and its Arts.* Melbourne: Fortuna Company.

Lassus, Jean. (1976). *The Early Christian and Byzantine World.* London: Hamlyn.

Milner-Gulland,Robin with Dejevsky, Nikolai. (1989.) *Atlas of Russia.*Oxford, England: Phaidon Press ltd.

Pavlyshyn, Marko. (1988). *One Thousand Years of Christianity in Ukraine.* Melbourne: Department of Slavic Languages, Monash University.

Pavlyshyn, Marko. (1986). *Ukrainian Settlement in Australia.* Melbourne: Department of Slavic Languages, Monash University.

Reid, Anna. (2001) *Borderland. A Journey Through the History of Ukraine.* London: Weidenfeld & Nicholson.

Wenhrynowycz, Rev. Stephan. (1990) *Willingly … no other choice.* Adelaide, Australia: Knyha Publishers. *(not translated)*

Embroidery

Diakiw O'Neill, Tania. (1984). *Ukrainian Embroidery Techniques.* Rochester NY: STO Publications.

Eaton, Gay. (2000). *Wessex Stitchery.* Georgesons, Auckland, New Zealand.

Gostelow, Mary. (1977). *The Complete International Book of Embroidery. New York:* Simon and Schuster.

Kara-Vasylieva T. (1983) *Folk Embroidery of the Poltava Region Ukraine. Kyviv. (not translated)*

Kmit, Ann. Luciow,Johanna. Luciow,Loretta. (1984). *Ukrainian Embroidery,* Minneapolis U.S.A: Van Nostrand Reinhold.

Kulynych-Stakhurska, Olena. (1996). *The Art of Ukrainian Embroidery.* Lviv.

Kutsenko, Maria. (1977) *Ukrainian Embroideries,* Melbourne: Spectrum Publications.

Klimova, Nina T. (1981) *Folk Embroidery of the U.S.S.R.* New York: Van Nostrand Reinhold.

Macyuk. O.O. Steparn M.H, (1984). *The Art of Embroidery Album.* Kyviv. *(not translated)*

Okuneva, Irene. Smith, Winifred. and S.N.E. *Embroidery,* March 1936, Vol IV: No. 2. London: The Embroiderers' Guild.

Paine, Sheila. (1990). *Embroidered Textiles, Traditional Patterns from Five Continents.* London: Thames & Hudson.

Ruryk, Nancy, R. (1982). *Ukrainian Embroidery Designs and Stitches.* Winnipeg, Manitoba: Ukrainian Women's Association of Canada.

Synge, Lanto. (2001). *Art of Embroidery.* Antique Collectors' Club U.K: The Royal School of Needlework.

TH. DE Dillmont, S.à.r.l. (undated) *D.M.C. Library Openwork Embroidery,* Mulhouse: France.